# Women of Achievement

## Julia Child

# Women of Achievement

Abigail Adams

Jane Addams

Susan B. Anthony

Tyra Banks

Clara Barton

Nellie Bly

Julia Child

Hillary Rodham
Clinton

Marie Curie

Ellen DeGeneres

Diana, Princess
of Wales

Amelia Earhart

Tina Fey

Ruth Bader Ginsburg

Joan of Arc

Angelina Jolie

Helen Keller

Madonna

Michelle Obama

Sandra Day O'Connor

Georgia O'Keeffe

Nancy Pelosi

Rachael Ray

Anita Roddick

Eleanor Roosevelt

Martha Stewart

Barbara Walters

Venus and Serena
Williams

*Women of Achievement*

# Julia Child

CHEF

**Dennis Abrams**

**CHELSEA HOUSE**
*An Infobase Learning Company*

**JULIA CHILD**

Chelsea House
An imprint of Infobase Learning
132 West 31st Street
New York, NY 10001

**Library of Congress Cataloging-in-Publication Data**
Abrams, Dennis, 1960–
  Julia Child, chef / by Dennis Abrams.
     p. cm. — (Women of achievement)
  Includes bibliographical references and index.
  ISBN 978-1-60413-912-9 (hardcover)
  1. Child, Julia—Juvenile literature. 2. Cooks—United States—Biography—
Juvenile literature. I. Title. II. Series.

  TX649.C47A65 2011
  641.5092—dc22
  [B]                              2011000039

Chelsea House books are available at special discounts when purchased in bulk quantities for businesses, associations, institutions, or sales promotions. Please call our Special Sales Department in New York at (212) 967-8800 or (800) 322-8755.

You can find Chelsea House on the World Wide Web
at http://www.infobaselearning.com.

Text design by Erik Lindstrom
Cover design by Ben Peterson and Alicia Post
Composition by EJB Publishing Services
Cover printed by Yurchak Printing, Landisville, Pa.
Book printed and bound by Yurchak Printing, Landisville, Pa.
Date printed: August 2011
Printed in the United States of America

10 9 8 7 6 5 4 3 2 1

This book is printed on acid-free paper.

All links and Web addresses were checked and verified to be correct at the time of publication. Because of the dynamic nature of the Web, some addresses and links may have changed since publication and may no longer be valid.

# CONTENTS

# Will Anybody Watch?

It was October 16, 1961. On that day, a new cookbook, a 732-page monument to the preparation of fine food entitled *Mastering the Art of French Cooking*, was published by Alfred A. Knopf. Two of its authors, Simone Beck (known to friends and colleagues alike as "Simca") and Louisette Bertholle, were French. The third author was a tall, ungainly 49-year-old American woman named Julia Child.

The concept of the book, teaching American housewives to prepare French food in their homes, had been a hard sell. The book's authors were unknown, and the idea was intimidating to women who had never cooked French food in their lives. In order for the book, which had taken nearly 10 years to complete, to sell, it would need more than just good reviews. The book's principal authors, Child and Beck, would have to help sell the book themselves, by going out on a book tour. They would make appearances in bookstores, on radio, and on television to help publicize and sell their book by persuading people to buy it.

They began with an appearance on a popular morning radio show that would be heard up and down the entire East Coast. It was their first time doing such an interview, but much to her surprise, Child discovered that she had no fears in being interviewed and no problem finding enough food-related topics to talk about for 20 minutes.

In fact, the radio appearance went so well that two days later, Child and Beck were invited to appear on the nation's top-rated morning news and entertainment program, *Today*. At that point, more than 4 million people nationwide watched the show. To Child and Beck, that translated into a lot of people who might be encouraged to buy their book.

Not only would they be interviewed, but they were asked to do a cooking demonstration as well. Given that they only had five minutes for their entire appearance, they decided that an omelet would be the most dramatic dish that they could quickly and easily prepare. The two arrived at the NBC studios at 5:00 in the morning on the day of the show, armed with all the equipment (knives, whips, bowls, and pans) and supplies they thought they might need.

What they did not anticipate, though, was the equipment that they found in the studio. Instead of a real stove, they would be using nothing more than a low-quality electric hot plate, which couldn't get nearly hot enough to cook an omelet to their liking. Fortunately, they had some time to experiment with it before going on the air. Each attempt to make an omelet, however, ended in failure. Finally, with just five minutes to air, they put the pan on the hot plate, turned it up as high as it would go, and, with only enough eggs left to prepare one omelet, hoped for the best.

The pleasures of cooking take sprout—brussels sprout, that is—in Julia Child's kitchen. Child's infectious personality won her, and the art of cooking, millions of fans. Who would have believed that, decades earlier, her classic book, *Mastering the Art of French Cooking*, had been a hard sell?

Fortunately, the interview with John Chancellor went well, and the last omelet turned out perfectly. For Child, who still did not even own a television, her first exposure to the world of broadcasting went better than expected. In those days, however, nobody imagined that there would actually be an audience interested in watching some-one cook on television. In fact, Child was more pleased with getting mentioned in *Life* magazine, having her and Beck's photos taken for *Vogue*, and being asked to write an article for *Home & Garden*—all more traditional ways to publicize a cookbook—than she had been by her television appearance.

Since the United States is a lot more than just New York City, and since they hoped to raise the level of cooking across the country through their book, the intrepid authors decided to take their act on the road. Not having a lot of money, they traveled to cities where they had friends who could put them up for the night and who could help arrange book signings at local bookstores, as well as lectures and cooking demonstrations. From New York, the authors went to Detroit, San Francisco, and finally Los Angeles, where they were able to stay with Child's father and stepmother before returning back to New York.

Publicizing the book involved long hours, and far more work than they had imagined. On one typical day, after being picked up in the morning at her sister Dort's house in Sausalito, California, they went to do an interview with the *Oakland Tribune*, then on to the Palace Hotel in San Francisco for a radio interview, then back to Sausalito, then on to Berkeley for more meetings, back to Sausalito, back again to San Francisco to attend a cocktail party given in their honor, and then, finally, to dinner with a woman who had promised to host a book party for them in Washington, D.C., and who promised to try to get the *Washington Post* to do an article on *Mastering the Art of French Cooking*.

These 15-hour days went on for a month and a half before everyone involved finally said they had had enough. Beck returned home to France, and Child returned home to Cambridge, Massachusetts, where she was greeted with the news that the work on her new kitchen was going well and that *Mastering the Art of French Cooking* had entered its third printing of 10,000 copies. To top it all off, she received her first royalty check for $2,610.85. Life, Child thought, would soon return to a more normal, quiet existence.

## AN INVITATION

The quiet life, however, would have to wait. Child received an invitation from a local public television station, WGBH, to appear on a show called *I've Been Reading*. She was given a full half hour to sit down with the show's host, Professor Albert Duhamel, to talk about food. Afterward, with the professor's assistance, she would demonstrate some techniques from her book. So after the regular interview, Child and Duhamel moved over to the show's "kitchen," where, with a proper hot plate that *she* provided, Child taught her host, a man with little to no culinary experience, how to cut and chop, how to "turn" a mushroom, how to beat egg whites, and how to make an omelet. The show went well, but Child assumed that this appearance would be the end of it.

It was not. WGBH received 27 letters from people saying that they wanted to see more. "Get that woman back on television," one letter said. "We want to see some more cooking!"[1] Twenty-seven letters may not seem like a lot, but to a small public television station in 1961, it was a remarkable response, indicating that, perhaps, there was an audience ready to learn how to master French cooking.

WGBH approached Child and asked her to put together three half-hour pilot (or test) programs on how to prepare French food in an American kitchen. Public television had never done anything of that nature before, and neither had Child, but she decided to take WGBH up on its offer. The publicity, she reasoned, could only help sales of her book. Besides, the reason she had written the book was to help teach people how to cook better and how to care about what they eat. What better way to spread the word than by teaching the art of French cooking on television?

In the summer of 1962, she taped the three pilot programs. In the first one she demonstrated how to make an omelet. In the second one, she showed viewers how to make the classic dish coq au vin—chicken braised in red wine. Finally, for the third show, she demonstrated how to make a soufflé—an egg dish, either savory or sweet, that is made light and fluffy through its use of beaten egg whites.

The first pilot episode was broadcast on July 26, and as Child and her husband, Paul, sat in front of their new television to watch, she was appalled by what she saw. As she wrote in *My Life in France*: "There I was, in black and white, a large woman sloshing eggs too quickly here, too slowly there, gasping, looking at the wrong camera while talking too loudly, and so on."[2]

Her husband reassured her, though, and told her that *he* thought she looked and sounded just like herself. Even Julia acknowledged later that "the cooking part went OK, but it was the performance of me, as talker and mover, that was not professional."[3] She even referred to the way she huffed and puffed and swooped and gasped across the TV screen by calling herself "Mrs. Steam Engine."

She wondered why anybody would want to watch her on television. Was there anyone interested in seeing her demonstrate French cooking? Given that the American diet at the time was dominated by canned foods, frozen foods, fast foods, and anything that could make it to the table quickly and easily, it did not seem likely that there would be a large enough audience.

It turned out, however, that people did want to watch her on television and did want to learn how to become better cooks, and in the process they turned Julia Child into one of the most beloved chefs and television personalities in history. They loved her for what she taught them: that good food was important, that taking the time to prepare a good meal was worthwhile, and that anyone willing to take the time to prepare a good meal *could* prepare a good meal.

Their feeling, though, went beyond that. When it came down to it, they loved Julia because she *was* Julia Child. As Laura Shapiro points out in her biography of Child:

> Julia Child was unlike any other celebrity in America. People gawked at her in restaurants, of course; greeted her joyfully on the streets; excitedly pointed her out to one another when they glimpsed her in an airport; and crowded into bookstores whenever she arrived to sign copies of her latest cookbook. None of this was out of the ordinary in the realms of fame. What was unique about Julia was the quality of the emotion she inspired, which was remarkably direct and pure. Julia attracted love, torrents of it, a steady outpouring of delighted love that began with the first pilot episode of *The French Chef* in 1962 and continued through and beyond her death in 2004. As a fan in California once wrote, "Whenever your name comes up, people smile."[4]

She did more than make people smile, however. Almost single-handedly, Julia Child led America from the culinary wilderness—away from tuna casseroles based on canned soups and into an exciting new world of fine cuisines and wines, a land where good food mattered. She taught Americans not to be intimidated by cooking, that cooking was a skill that could be learned like any other, and she encouraged them to believe that home cooking could, in fact, be sophisticated cooking.

Without her influence, it seems unlikely that the cookbook industry would be as large as it is today, that entire television channels would be devoted to food and cook-

Julia Child, shown on the set of *The French Chef* in 1970, taped the first pilot episodes for the series in 1962. At the time, it was unclear if there was an audience for a cooking show on television. With her programs, however, Child helped to transform the culinary experience in the United States, teaching people to appreciate well-prepared food.

ing, and that cooking competitions like *Top Chef* and *Hell's Kitchen* would be as avidly watched as sports competitions. Without Child, gourmet food stores like Williams-Sonoma and Sur La Table might not exist, the kitchen in your home would not have the equipment and tools that is has now, and the very food you had for dinner might be quite different.

Her impact, obviously, was enormous. But how did she do it? This tall, curiously voiced, utterly unique person transformed America's culinary landscape, but she had never eaten proper French food until she was 36. She became enamored with food and earned her certificate from culinary school only months before she turned 40, learning the skills that would make her the legendary "French Chef" to millions of Americans. Although as a girl she "had zero interest in the stove"[5] and didn't even see the point of learning *how* to cook, she became the woman who would teach generations of Americans the proper way to cook, and also the importance of both cooking and dining well.

It is a story of discovery, of a woman finding herself and her passion, and then finding a way to share that passion with the world. It is the story of how Julia Carolyn McWilliams, through a combination of drive, determination, talent, and love of what she was doing, transformed herself into Julia Child, the French Chef, and in the process, helped to transform America.

# Childhood and Beyond

She was born Julia Carolyn McWilliams in Pasadena, California, on August 15, 1912. It was, as Noël Riley Fitch notes in her biography of Child, a different era from the one we know today. It was still a time "when telephone lines were shared by several families, and horse-drawn wagons delivered ice, vegetables, milk, and eggs daily to the house."[1]

Julia was the first-born child of John McWilliams and Julia Carolyn Weston. Her father was the son of a man, also named John, who had traveled from Illinois to California to pan for gold and made the family fortune by investing in California mineral rights and Arkansas rice fields. Julia's father, a graduate of Princeton University and a conservative Republican, managed his father's large landholdings and investments, and eventually became vice president of the J.G. Boswell Company, a major developer and land-owner in California.

Her mother, known as "Caro," also came from money. Caro's family could trace its ancestry back to eleventh-century England and had lived in Plymouth Colony. One of the seven children of the founder of the Weston Paper Company, Caro was a free-spirited graduate of Smith College, a woman who supplied her family with love and a lively sense of humor, while her husband provided the discipline and encouraged his children—another daughter, Dorothy, and a son, John—to contribute to the public good. Julia grew up to combine the best qualities of them both.

Her childhood was close to idyllic, with time spent in both her parents' house and in a three-story house on Pasadena's Euclid Avenue owned by the McWilliams grand-parents. While Julia had strong memories of the "delicious broiled chicken and wonderful doughnuts"[2] made by her grandmother, some of her earliest happy memories involved Christmas:

> First we'd do the stockings, which were filled with candy canes and apples and a lot of small presents. Then we'd have a big breakfast with eggs and bacon and fruit, but we'd all be panting for gifts. One year Santa Claus left his pipe on the mantel. It was a meerschaum filled with tobacco and had been smoked. We children marveled over it for years.[3]

The family was wealthy enough to have a large number of servants. There was an upstairs maid who kept the house clean. There was a Scottish nurse named Annie Hignett, whose responsibility was taking care of the youngest daughter, Dorothy. There was an Irish cook, and there was even a gardener named Clearwater, who was in charge of keeping up the acre (0.4 hectare) of land surrounding the house, the orchard, the garden, the chickens, and the grass tennis court.

Given this, it would be natural to assume that Julia grew up eating nothing but the finest and fanciest gourmet foods possible. That, however, was not the case. As she often said in interviews, "It was good, plain New England food, the kind my mother had back in Massachusetts."[4] This meant that the meat was cooked until it was well done, the vegetables were those available seasonally, and instead of wine, water was served in long-stemmed, gold-rimmed glasses.

At most times, the food was prepared by the cook. On her night off, Julia's mother would step into the kitchen, to make her family's famous baking powder biscuits and Welsh rarebit, a dish featuring a tasty sauce of melted cheese served over toast or biscuits. In those days, food wasn't necessarily taken seriously as something to be enjoyed and savored. It was a necessity, something to provide fuel and nutrition for the body.

As for Julia, it wasn't so much what she ate as the amount she could eat. "I was always hungry," she recalled later. "I had the appetite of a wolf."[5] Her main goal for her first 30 years of eating, as her husband Paul Child later said, was simply to eat as much as possible.

## GROWING UP

Growing up in Pasadena, Julia led what can only be considered a normal, if somewhat privileged, childhood. Her parents were, as biographer Noël Riley Fitch noted, both "socially active and athletic . . . who loved the outdoors and belonged to several country clubs."[6] Julia was encouraged to be active as well, to play outdoors with her friends, to organize activities, and most importantly, to keep busy and do something with her life.

As the oldest child, Julia spent her childhood testing the boundaries of her parents' authority, even experimenting with smoking cigarettes until her father offered her and her siblings a $1,000 bond if they promised not to smoke at least until they turned 21. "We did not smoke after that," Child claimed. "I kept my bargain. At one minute after midnight on my twenty-first birthday, I began smoking and smoked for thirty years, at least one to two packs of cigarettes every day."[7]

Her schools were private schools. She attended Mrs. Davies's Montessori school, an ungraded, somewhat experimental school, from the age of four. From fourth grade through ninth grade, she attended the Polytechnic School, where, because of her height if for no other reason, she was considered to be a great athlete (although one classmate had strong memories of Julia constantly tripping over things). She was popular, acted in school plays, and, although she had no specific goals for herself in mind, wrote in her diary that she was "like no one else" and "meant for something" special.[8] What, she must have asked herself, could that something special be?

While her friends did not know what it would be either, they were certain it wouldn't be acting. Julia loved to perform, but because of her height and her voice, it seemed unlikely that theater or performing would be in her future. Her voice, well described by Fitch, was unlike any other:

A high-pitched, breathy sound drew Julia's vowels up and down a musical scale in such a way that her sentences turned into arias. When she was excited, her voice sounded like a honking falsetto. When she was ecstatic, her voice might chortle, guffaw, crack, or half yodel.[9]

(continues on page 22)

# M.F.K. FISHER

If Julia Child was the technician who taught Americans how to cook, M.F.K. Fisher was the philosopher, the poet, who through her writing taught us how to love food, and how to appreciate it as something as essential and meaningful as love, as life itself.

Born Mary Frances Kennedy (M.F.K.) on July 3, 1908 (just four years before Child), she had an all-American childhood in California, before making her escape by marrying Alfred Fisher at the age of 19 and fleeing to Dijon, France, where (again like Child) she discovered the joys of France and fine French food.

There would be other loves for Fisher and other cities in California and France and Switzerland, and her writing tells the story of that life—of the meals, the cooking, the kitchens, the men, the places, and the way in which they were all unalterably entwined.

It is doubtful that anybody, ever, could write more lovingly, more perceptively, more excitingly about food and life than Fisher. The poet W.H. Auden said that he didn't know of anybody in the United States who wrote better prose. Just this example will show how her descriptive powers can make something as mundane as a bowl of mashed potatoes extraordinary:

> I was alone, which seems to be indicated for many such sensual rites. The potatoes were light, whipped to a firm cloud with rich hot milk, faintly yellow from ample butter. I put them in a big warmed bowl, made a dent about the size of a respectable coffee cup, and filled it to the brim with catsup from a large, full vulgar bottle that stood beside my table mat where a wineglass would be at an ordinary, commonplace, everyday banquet. Mine was, as I have said, delicious.*

Author M.F.K. Fisher, shown in her office in Sonoma, California, in 1971, taught people to love food and view it as being as essential to life as love. W.H. Auden declared that no one in the United States could write prose as well as Fisher.

For the last 20 years of her life, M.F.K. Fisher lived in "Last House," a home built for her in one of California's vineyards. She died there on June 22, 1992, at the age of 83.

---

* Betty Fussell, *Masters of American Cookery: The American Food Revolution and the Chefs Who Shaped It*. New York: Times Books, 1983, p. 23.

*(continued from page 19)*

## THE KATHARINE BRANSON SCHOOL

After graduating from the Polytechnic School in June 1927, Julia was sent to boarding school for her high school years, to the Katharine Branson School in Marin County in northern California. The school was designed to give California girls a traditional New England education, the kind that Julia's mother had had when she was growing up. This education was designed to prepare them to go to a women's college on the East Coast—hopefully one of the famous "Seven Sisters" schools.

But the education she was given at Branson was largely wasted on Julia. She did well in school but did not put in the effort necessary to truly excel. Her interests lay largely outside of the classroom: parties at the beach, leading friends on hiking trips, athletic events, and playing the title role in one of the school plays, *Michael, the Sword Eater*.

She was an extremely popular student who was seen as a natural leader, and she graduated not with the highest academic honors, but as Branson's First Citizen. A fellow student and friend remembered what she was like at that time:

> She was . . . gangly, a little awkward, standing tall but stooping slightly to look benignly down on the rest of us. She was serious about life, but had a unique way of seeing the humor in incidents, and expressing it in her deep, rather thick manner of speaking. She wasn't trying to be funny. In fact she was very modest and unassuming, totally lacking in exhibitionism. She was just reacting naturally to a situation. . . . What she was thinking, she said, and it was usually very apt. And often very funny. . . . She wasn't attention seeking, nor aggressive, nor competitive, nor ambitious. . . . She is just herself.[10]

Indeed, Julia McWilliams was far from ambitious. She gave in to her mother's expectations and, after graduating from Branson, went to her mother's alma mater, Smith College. As her enrollment form listing her vocational plans indicates, however, she wasn't expecting to do much. "No occupation decided; marriage preferable."[11]

## SMITH COLLEGE

After four years at Smith College, there was *still* no occupation decided upon. During her time there she studied just enough to keep herself from getting bored and kicked out of school, and she decided to major in history for the simple reason that "it had more options."[12] She also took classes in French, developed a fondness for writing, lived on all-American dormitory food, made friends, and drank too much during her senior year. Years later, Child described her time at Smith as being done to please her mother and as the period when she began, very slowly, to grow up.

When she graduated with a B.A. in history in 1934, she was as without direction as when she had enrolled. Her hometown paper in Pasadena announced her graduation, saying, "She will return here after graduation and will pass the summer with her family at the McWilliams beach house at San Malo."[13] What she would do beyond that was still an unanswered question.

## SEARCHING

As she said in a 1989 interview, "Middle-class women did not have careers. You were to marry and have children and be a nice mother. You didn't go out and do anything."[14]

Her first year after graduating from Smith was spent doing exactly that—not going out and doing anything. She helped to take care of her mother, who was suffering from high blood pressure, played piano, socialized with friends, and studied for and received membership in the Junior

League, *the* social organization for young women of her age. A friend, Gay Bradley, later remembered their time in the Junior League:

> Julia was the center of attention and activity; when we were all together she was always the focus, always the funny one, always the clown (of course she had her serious side); when she was little she was always the first one throwing butter at the ceiling, the ringleader . . . always the kind of person people follow because she had great magnetism.[15]

But the life of a proper young woman in Pasadena, biding her time with Junior League activities until she managed to snag a husband, was not enough for her. She grew restless living at home and informed the vocational guidance office at Smith that she wanted a literary career, perhaps writing for a newspaper or a magazine, or even writing a novel. She returned to Massachusetts to take a stenography class at the Packard Commercial School and then moved to New York City, where, along with two friends from Smith, she took an apartment and went out in search of a career.

It was the fall of 1935, and, initially, things did not go well. Child was unable to get an interview with America's premier literary magazine, *The New Yorker*, and, despite the stenography course, she failed the entry-level typing test at *Newsweek*. Finally, though, and much to her relief, she landed a job in the advertising department at W. & J. Sloane, a Fifth Avenue furniture store.

She worked there for a year and a half, writing press releases for New York newspapers describing the new products at Sloane's. She went into the job knowing nothing about furniture, but, as she told the Smith College alumni office, "I am learning quite a bit about store management and interior decoration. In fact, I couldn't be more pleased."[16]

Child learned that she had a gift for writing, even when describing somewhat dubious products, as one draft proves:

> When you have put your all into a party, and struggled over making sandwiches that are chic and dashing as well as tastey [sic], it is terribly deflating to have their pretty figures ruined by guests who must peak [sic] inside each 'wich to see what it's made of.

The solution, available only at Sloane's, was ingenious and scary at the same time:

> Sandwich indicators—wooden picks which you stick in the sandwich plate, nicely shaped and painted. There is "Humpty-Dumpty" for egg, a rat in a cage for cheese, a dog, boat, and pig for meat, fish, and ham. And it seems like a very sound idea.[17]

It does seem unlikely, however, that, even during this period of her life, Julia Child could have been fully charmed by the idea of identifying a cheese sandwich with a rat-shaped toothpick.

Her bosses, though, must have been happy with her work: Her starting salary of $20 a week was soon raised to $35. At the same time, and for the first time, she had fallen in love with a young man. However, the man, named Tom Johnston, ended their relationship with a letter in the fall of 1936 informing her that he did not love her. Heartbroken, she returned home to Pasadena in May 1937, giving up on her dream of a literary life in New York.

She was greeted by an ongoing family tragedy. Her beloved mother, Caro, died on July 21, 1937, with Julia at her side, from complications from high blood pressure. It was a huge blow to Julia, who wrote in her diary:

I had a feeling, I guess I really knew before I came out here that she would die. I knew it, I knew she'd be dead by this fall, but I didn't realize it. I could have been much nicer to her. I could have been with her more.[18]

With her father relying on her for companionship and emotional support, Julia stayed in Pasadena, returning to the social and volunteer activities she had fled from two years earlier. The Smith College vocational office told her about job opportunities in New York and Paris, but she refused them. Instead, she tried her hand at fashion writing. She became a monthly columnist for a little-known magazine, *Coast*, which had the advantage of being published in San Francisco by friends of the family.

She hated it, later referring to it as a "loathsome business,"[19] and was frankly relieved when the magazine went bankrupt in mid-1939. Julia then went to work for the Beverly Hills branch of her old employer, W. & J. Sloane, becoming its advertising manager, setting up the office, and being responsible for the entire store's advertising. She was fired after just four months, though, after making a serious error of judgment on the job.

Julia was not particularly upset about getting fired, knowing in her heart that she did not have the necessary knowledge of business. But she *also* knew that the years she had spent at home had been an important period in her life, a period when she began to, ever so slowly, become an adult with a better sense of herself. She also came to the realization, after nearly marrying and then rejecting Harrison Chandler, a member of the wealthy and powerful family that owned the *Los Angeles Times*, that finding a husband and settling down to start a family were no longer her top priorities. As she wrote in her diary:

And thank heaven I am getting over that fear and contempt of single maidenhood. . . . I am quite content to be the way I am—and feel quite superior to many a wedded mouse. By god—I can do what I want![20]

With the coming of World War II, Julia, like millions of women around the country, would soon have the opportunity to do what she wanted. She began her war work in the fall of 1941, volunteering at the local office of the Red Cross. Then, after the Japanese attacked the U.S. naval base at Pearl Harbor in Hawaii, which brought the United States directly into the war, she joined the Aircraft Warning Service and took the civil service exam. She even filled out applications to join the branches of the navy and army that were available for women. But at six feet two inches (1.88 meters), much to her disappointment, she learned that she was too tall for the military.

Still wanting to do her part, she moved to Washington, D.C., where she got a job typing index cards at the U.S. Information Center in the Office of Wartime Intelligence. The job was boring beyond belief, and she quit after just three months. Her next job, however, would be the one that would change her life forever.

She went to work for the Office of Strategic Services (OSS), which was headed by General William "Wild Bill" Donovan. The office, the forerunner of today's Central Intelligence Agency (CIA), was a network of espionage and intelligence operations throughout Europe and the Far East. It was, to put it bluntly, America's spy agency.

Does this mean that Julia was a real-life cloak and dagger spy? Hardly. She started work there doing exactly what she had done in the Office of Wartime Intelligence, typing and filing her days away. But when "Wild Bill" Donovan began

William "Wild Bill" Donovan was the head of the Office of Strategic Services, the nation's spy agency, during World War II. Julia McWilliams went to work as a clerk for the OSS during the war, and when Donovan sought volunteers to work in OSS offices overseas, she seized the opportunity.

to look for volunteers to work in OSS offices overseas, Julia jumped at the chance. Here, at last, was something new and exciting. As biographer Laura Shapiro summarized it, "Here was a chance to travel someplace completely improbable, someplace way, way off the map of her life to date."[21]

The time had come when Junior League member Julia McWilliams could, at last, do what she wanted. She put in a request to go to India, and she set sail on a troop ship in March 1944. Julia often reflected that "I got an awfully late start."[22] Now, at last, at the age of 31, her life was truly beginning.

# Finding Her Passions

As it turned out, Julia only thought she was going to India. En route, the orders were changed. Instead of India, she would be stationed in Ceylon, a teardrop-shaped island (now known as Sri Lanka) just off India's southern coast. After arriving in the capital city of Colombo, she was sent to the hill town of Kandy, where Lord Louis Mountbatten was directing the South East Asia Command.

It was a gorgeous place to be (Lord Mountbatten once described Kandy as probably the most beautiful spot in the world), although working conditions were primitive at best. "Our office is a series of palm-thatched huts connected by cement walks, surrounded by native workmen and barbed wire"[1] was how Julia described it in a letter to her family.

Based in the former tea plantation that had become the Office of Strategic Services headquarters, Julia settled into work, which turned out to be, largely, the same paperwork that she had been doing in Washington. Her job was to set up and then maintain the Registry, an assignment that she was forced to do on her own until an assistant was sent in months later to help. All classified documents pertaining to intelligence in the China-Burma-India theater of war went through the Registry, and Julia was the one who created a system that made the flood of information manageable and readily available to those who needed it.

It was a life very different from the ones she had known in Pasadena, at Smith, and in New York City. There were tarantulas, termites, gigantic cockroaches, torrential rains, and tropical heat, and elephants performed much of the heavy work. Yet, Julia, despite her protected and privileged background, thrived in Ceylon, feeling fully independent for the first time in her life, doing work that truly mattered for the first time in her life, and waking up every morning to a life that was an adventure.

The adventure went well beyond the work she was doing and beyond the exotic location she was doing it in. From her office window, she had a direct view into the window of a fellow OSS employee, the head of the Visual Presentation Group, the man who had created a secret war room and drew the maps for Admiral Mountbatten. His name was Paul Child.

## MEETING PAUL CHILD

While Julia McWilliams, because of her careful upbringing, was still relatively naïve and inexperienced ("a grown-up little girl,"[2] was Paul's first impression of her), Paul Child was a man who, in the words of Laura Shapiro, "had lived like a character in a boys' adventure story."[3]

Servicemen used elephants to visit the Mahaweli Ganga river in Kandy, Ceylon, in November 1944. Julia McWilliams was stationed at the Office of Strategic Services headquarters in Kandy. The world there was much different from what she was accustomed to back in the United States. She was beginning to develop her independence.

His father, who had worked in the Astrophysical Observatory at the Smithsonian Institution, had died in 1902, when Paul and his twin brother, Charlie, were just a few months old. It fell to their mother, Bertha Cushing Child, to raise the two boys and their sister on her own. She moved them back to Boston, where she eked out a living as a singer, performing with the Boston Symphony Orchestra and the Handel and Haydn Society.

The twins were taught to play the violin and the cello, their sister was assigned the piano, and as soon as they were proficient, their mother put them all to work, booking the family for performances as "Mrs. Child and the Children." This, however, was just the first of the many careers of Paul Child.

After finishing high school, he went to work in a stained-glass shop, learning how to cut and glaze the glass, before deciding to head out on his own to see the world. He worked as a waiter in Hollywood. He was a tutor for an American family living in Italy. He was a wood-carver in Paris. He was a teacher at a series of private schools throughout New England.

He was a black belt in judo, an accomplished photographer, painter, gardener, and poet, and a man passionately interested in finding out how the world worked, through images, design, and language. He was an experienced and erudite man, who for 17 years had lived, in Paris and Cambridge, with a brilliantly accomplished woman 20 years his senior who died of cancer in 1942 and left him convinced that, as he wrote in a letter to his brother, "I am really spoiled for other women and I realize it over and over."[4] Given his background and tastes, falling in love with the awkward, unworldly, and still immature Julia McWilliams seemed to him an impossibility.

But for Julia, Paul Child was like no one she had ever met before. She noticed him just days after her arrival at

Kandy, and by May 1944, she was writing about him in her diary:

> I have a nice time with the office men—not *Whee*, but pleasant. There is Paul Child, an artist who, when I first saw him, I thought as not at all nice looking. He is about 40 [he was 42, she almost 32], has light hair which is *not* on top, an unbecoming blond mustache and a long unbecoming nose. But he is very composed. I find him both pleasant, comfortable, and very mentally get-at-able. We have dinner frequently and go to the movies.[5]

For his part, Paul was mostly impressed with her amiable good nature and great legs. He enjoyed spending time with her, but in a letter to his brother, he made clear why Julia McWilliams would never become the woman of his dreams: "Her mind is potentially good, but she is an extremely sloppy thinker."[6] Child blamed this lack of clear thinking on her wealthy, conservative background, a background that forced her to see life through the eyes of her family back home rather than independently.

In his eyes, though, she did have one saving grace. She *knew* that she came from a privileged conservative background, and one reason she was in Ceylon was to move beyond her family, to discover new things, learn new ideas, and see the world from different perspectives. She was eager to learn, and it would fall to Paul Child to help encourage and inspire her to broaden her horizons.

## ON TO CHINA

While Paul Child played his role in expanding Julia's intellectual and emotional horizons, her geographic horizons were about to expand as well. After 10 months in Ceylon, Julia, along with many of the other OSS employees stationed at Kandy, was being moved to China. Paul was transferred at the end of 1944. On March 8, 1945, Julia followed, flying to Calcutta, India (a city she hated), and on to Kunming, China, where she would set up and operate the new OSS Registry.

The flight across "the Hump," which took her and the other 30 passengers over the soaring Himalaya Mountains, was, with little doubt, the most dangerous and risky of her wartime experiences. Julia, though, took it in stride. While many of her fellow passengers spent their time in prayer as their unpressurized and unheated plane made its way over the mountain peaks, Child remained absorbed in her book, oblivious to the danger surrounding her.

After a tumultuous three-hour flight, the pilot found a hole in the clouds and made a steep descent before landing at Roger Queen airport. While the other passengers thanked God for their safe arrival, Julia could hardly wait to see what would happen next, as her friend Betty MacDonald remembered:

> Julia, climbing down first, looked over the low, red hills and the curling rooftop of a small temple near the field, received a cheerful "Ting hao" greeting from some red-cheeked children, and turned back to her fellow passengers. "It looks *just* like China," she told us.[7]

It is all too easy to imagine the look of pleasure on her face and the delighted tone in her voice when she made this announcement.

Julia loved China and loved being reunited with Paul. For his part, Paul loved China and was happy to be reunited with Julia, but he still thought of her only as a friend, not as a possible wife. Still, by being brought together in a foreign land, they spent a great deal of time with each other, and their friendship continued to deepen.

Much of that time was spent searching out great, authentic Chinese food. The food cooked by the Chinese staff working in the barracks—"rice, potatoes, canned tomatoes and water buffalo"[8]—was not satisfying to Julia, and even less so to Paul, whose years of living in France had given him a taste for fine cuisine. Paul often told Julia about the food he had eaten in France and about French cuisine in general. To both of them, Chinese food at its best was a more than acceptable substitute.

Julia began to learn about food, to develop her palate, and to be able to taste the difference between good food and great food. She cultivated a fondness for northern, Peking-style Chinese cooking. As she learned to speak more and more intelligently about food (as well as other topics), Paul's interest in her continued to grow.

Still, though, even as the war came to an end in the late summer of 1945, he only saw her as a "friend" and not a "girlfriend," as he explained in a letter to his twin brother, Charlie:

> Over the 18 months or more that I have known Julia, I have become extremely fond of her. She is really a good friend, and though limited . . . she still is understanding, warm, funny, and darling. . . . [S]he is a woman with whom I take much comfort, and she has helped me over many a rough spot by just simple love and niceness.[9]

Julia, on the other hand, was in love. With the end of the war, questions arose as to how their relationship could continue. On October 1, 1945, President Harry Truman announced the end of the OSS, and their futures, both in terms of their careers and their personal lives, were

Much the happy couple in 1975, Julia Child and her husband, Paul, performed an informal recital in their home in Cambridge, Massachusetts. In the beginning, however, their relationship slowly evolved during their time together in the OSS. Even at the end of World War II, Paul only saw Julia as a "friend," not a "girlfriend."

completely up in the air. In her journal, Julia questioned whether their relationship had a chance:

> I am not the woman for him as I am not intellectual. He is probably not the man for me as he is not constant nor essentially vigorous enough. . . . But his sensitiveness and the fact that we can talk about anything and there are no conventional barriers in

thought communication make him a warm and lovable friend.[10]

The two would soon be sent back to America. With Julia returning to her home in Pasadena and Paul based on the East Coast in Washington, what form would their relationship take?

Julia McWilliams spent the first six months of 1946 in Pasadena, living a life that must have seemed incredibly humdrum after her experiences in Asia. In those days before affordable long-distance phone calls, before Facebook, and before texting, she and Paul communicated by writing long letters to each other. His feelings for her continued to grow deeper, and he made plans to go to California in the summer.

As for Julia, her feelings for Paul already existed, and she knew she wanted to marry him. She read the books that he suggested, she studied semantics and psychology because of his interest in the subjects, and she began to read the *Washington Post* and the *New York Times*, because of his interest in politics.

And if the old saying was true, that the way to a man's heart was through his stomach, Julia was determined to use food and cooking as a way to win Paul's heart. "Paul's mother was a good cook, and he had lived in France. If I was going to catch him, I would have to learn to cook," she wrote years later.[11]

She tried to learn on her own for weeks, writing to Paul about her failures and occasional successes, before realizing that she simply was not a born cook. As biographer Laura Shapiro pointed out, she was not one of those talented few who were able to walk into a kitchen, grab some ingredients, and come up with a wonderful dish. Cookbooks helped, but most were badly written and could only take her so far. If she wanted to learn to cook well, she would have to go to school.

So along with a friend, she signed up for cooking classes at the Hillcliff School of Cookery, run by two rather elderly English ladies named Mary Hill and Irene Radcliffe. Julia discovered that she thoroughly enjoyed the process of learning to cook, and she eagerly came home from class ready to practice what she had learned. Sometimes she succeeded, as in the dinner party she threw for 12, featuring three kinds of hors d'oeuvres, steak and kidney pie, and peas cooked the French way, with lettuce.

Other times, she failed. There was the time a duck exploded in the oven because she had forgotten to prick the skin. There was the time she got up early one morning to make a big breakfast for the family and yet, two hours later, nothing was ready to eat and she was in hysterics. Years later, she was still angry with herself about that one: "The kitchen was a mess, and they came in and hovered over me, and the coffee fell on the floor and burned them, and they made rude remarks, and I threw them out and burst into tears."[12]

Regardless of whether her experiments were a success or a failure, Julia shared them in her letters to Paul. It was food that became their connection, the topic that brought them together in ways that had seemed impossible during

## IN HER OWN WORDS

Julia Child on her late start as a cook:

I was 32 when I started cooking; up until then, I just ate.*

---

* "Julia Child quotes," Think Exist, http://thinkexist.com/ quotation/i_was-when_i_started_cooking-up_until_then- i_just/210644.html.

their time in Asia. Paul arrived in Pasadena on July 7, and just days later, the pair climbed into Julia's Buick to make the cross-country trip back to the East Coast together. It was a long trip, one designed to either bring them together or drive them apart. By the time they reached Niagara Falls, Paul had made a decision. He was in love with Julia as much as she was in love with him.

Perhaps surprisingly, what Paul fell in love with was not so much her love of cooking or her willingness to grow intellectually, but her *character*. What Paul Child finally fell in love with were the same traits that audiences would later fall in love with as well. In a letter to his brother, he wrote:

> She *never* puts on an act. She frankly likes to eat and use her senses. . . . She has a cheerful, gay humor with considerable gusto. . . . She loves life and all its phenomena. . . . She has deep-seated charm and human warmth which I have been fascinated to see work on people of all sorts, from the sophisticates of San Francisco to the mining and cattle folk of the Northwest. . . . She tells the truth.[13]

## GETTING MARRIED

The two decided to get married quickly, setting the date for September 1, 1946. Just one day before the ceremony, on their way to an engagement party, their car was struck by an approaching truck that had lost its brakes. Paul suffered bruised ribs and was thrown from the car. Julia recounted that she "hit the windshield and was thrown out the door and my shoes came off. I was knocked out and covered with blood from a head wound."[14]

The car was totaled, and, as they later determined, it had only been a matter of luck and inches that had kept them alive. Despite their injuries, Julia insisted on going ahead with the wedding. "We were married in stitches," Paul said, "me on a cane and Julia full of glass."[15] Because the couple had decided that their cross-country road trip would serve as their honeymoon, and since Paul needed to return to work, they moved to Washington, D.C.

They lived there for nearly two years. Paul spent those years trying to figure out a new career course, while his bride settled into the life of a Washington, D.C., hostess, all the time continuing to try to hone her cooking skills. It was not easy, especially since by even trying to learn to cook "fine cuisine," Julia Child was going against the culinary winds.

It was the era of frozen foods, canned foods, and convenience foods. It was the era when women were told that cooking was somehow a nuisance, that faster preparation was better, and that taking the time to prepare good food was somehow a waste. It was a time when magazines like the *Ladies' Home Journal* promised to teach its readers to "Learn to Cook in Five Meals!,"[16] which was simply a question of opening cans, packages of Jell-O, and bags of frozen vegetables. It seemed to many that America's favorite foods were instant coffee, instant pudding, and casseroles made from canned soup, canned tuna, and potato chips.

Julia Child, though, was having none of it. She wanted to learn to cook, and she wanted to learn to cook well. She read cookbooks, subscribed to *Gourmet* magazine, and practiced, practiced, practiced. Sometimes her dishes worked; sometimes they didn't. Regardless, she was determined to succeed. As a friend recalled, "Julia at that time was not a great cook, but she wanted to know how food worked. She wanted to know about everything."[17]

Once again, though, career opportunities were changing her life. Paul Child's career with the State Department, which had had its up and downs, was once again on the upswing. In the summer of 1948, he was told that he was being posted to Paris, where he would be the exhibits officer at the United States Information Service. He was thrilled to be returning to Paris, his favorite city on Earth, and to have the opportunity to share it with his wife.

Now 36 years old, Julia Child and her husband, Paul, boarded the SS *America* on October 27, 1948, along with 14 pieces of luggage, trunks, and their car. After a stormy five-day journey across the Atlantic, they docked at Le Havre, where they claimed their car and set off on the road to Paris, a road that, unbeknownst to them, would lead directly to Julia Child's culinary destiny.

# Finding
# Her Career

Life, if one is lucky, can be filled with "a-ha" moments, moments that can lead to realizations about one's self, about one's life, about one's purpose. For Julia Child, one such moment occurred the very same afternoon she arrived in France.

After loading their car with all their belongings, Julia and Paul Child set out on the road to Paris. The road led through the French countryside, where, as when she first arrived in China, Julia could only think to herself that it looked just like the France of her dreams.

While France still bore the scars of the recent war, life was returning to normal, and Julia was enthralled with the sight of the deeply green countryside and fields, the old men still driving horse-and-buggies, the peasant women still dressed in black. It was all different (even the telephone poles were a different size and shape from those she knew in America) and so beautiful that, before it was even time for lunch, she was falling in love with France.

They stopped in the city of Rouen, known for its famous cathedral with magnificent stained-glass windows. At 12:30 p.m., they pulled into La Place du Vieux Marche, the city square famous for being the site where Joan of Arc was burned at the stake on May 30, 1431. There, at the Restaurant La Couronne ("The Crown"), built in a quarter-timbered medieval house in 1345 and known as France's oldest inn, Julia Child had a meal that transformed her concept of what fine food could be. It was a meal that quite literally changed her life.

French food is based on using the finest local seasonal ingredients. Since Rouen is close to the coast, the meal was largely seafood. It began with oysters, still plump and briny from the sea, served with Chablis, a crisp, dry white wine that is a classic partner for raw seafood. The next course was also seafood, *sole meunière*, selected especially by Paul. Nearly 30 years later, Child described the dish in her book *From Julia Child's Kitchen*, and it is evident that the memory of the dish, and the way it made her feel, was still as fresh as if she had just eaten it:

> In came our fish on a large oval platter, a whole big flat sole for the two of us. It was handsomely browned and still sputteringly hot under its coating of chopped parsley, and around it swirled a goodly amount of golden Normandy butter. It was heaven to eat, the flesh so very fresh, with its delicate yet definite texture and taste that blended marvelously with the browned butter sauce. I was quite overwhelmed.[1]

Restaurant La Couronne, on La Place du Vieux Marche in Rouen, is known as France's oldest inn. There, in 1948, on the day she and Paul Child arrived in France, Julia Child had a meal of sole meunière that changed how she thought about food. "It was heaven to eat," Julia wrote.

The meal ended with a simple salad, crème fraîche, and coffee. Child savored every bite, enjoying each dish as though she were discovering food for the first time. In a way, she was. Food of that quality, the kind of food that the French took for granted, was unavailable to most people in the United States.

It was a revelation to Julia that food, so simply and yet carefully prepared, could be so utterly delicious. For her, driving out of Rouen and past its towering cathedral, it was the meal that had provided the truly inspiring experience. "The whole experience was an opening up of the soul and spirit for me. . . . I was hooked, and for life, as it has turned out."[2] In many ways, her career, her goal in life, would be to help provide Americans with the tools to replicate her experience for themselves, from the comfort of their own kitchens.

Settling into life in Paris, she quickly fell in love with the city, its people, its food, and its way of life. She never tired of eating at restaurants, watching whole families celebrating themselves and their lives with fine food. "We keep

## IN HER OWN WORDS

Julia Child on finding her creative outlet through food:

> Some people like to paint, or do gardening, or build a boat in the basement. Other people get a tremendous pleasure out of the kitchen, because cooking is just as creative as drawing, or woodcarving, or music.*

* Jone Johnson Lewis, "Julia Child quotes," About.com, http://womenshistory.about.com/od/juliachild/a/julia_child.htm.

Shoppers crowded the street market on Rue Mouffetard in Paris one morning in 1963. After arriving in Paris, Julia Child spent her days walking the streets, exploring the city. She discovered the street markets, with fresh foods of all varieties available, and for her, she found a new way of shopping for food.

being reminded of the Orient," she wrote in a letter home. "Possibly because both are cultivated old civilizations, who enjoy and have integrated the physical and the cultural things in living."[3]

As Paul settled into work, she settled into her life, taking French lessons at Berlitz and setting up house at their third-floor apartment at 81, rue de l'Université, on the Left Bank of the river Seine. Armed with a map and a dictionary, she spent her days walking the streets of Paris, eager to explore and absorb all the city had to offer.

Everything she saw, everything she smelled, everything she tasted was new and fresh and exhilarating. She roamed the markets, a series of stalls where one person might be selling brie, another fresh chicken, another sausage, another mushrooms. She would walk along, sampling as she went, tasting and learning how to buy the best cheeses, fruits ("great big juicy pears"[4]), and meats she could find. It was a new way of shopping for food, and one she learned to love, praising in a letter home "those lovely, intimate, delicious, mouth-watering, friendly, fascinating places."[5]

But as much as she loved the city and loved exploring its various neighborhoods, markets, and alleyways, as much as she loved coming back to her apartment to prepare the food she had purchased, it wasn't enough. She needed something to *do* with her life.

For a brief time, as hard as it may be to believe, she considered becoming a hat maker. She took a few classes and even tried her hand at designing a hat and a dress that she wore to a wedding, before realizing that fashion wasn't for her. Fortunately, Paul Child came up with a solution.

He had been discussing Julia's "problem" with a friend, who asked him, "What does Julia like?" Paul Child thought about it for a moment before answering, "She likes to *eat*."[6] The solution was obvious. In the fall of 1949, Julia Child enrolled in one of France's most prestigious culinary schools, Le Cordon Bleu.

## BACK TO SCHOOL

Le Cordon Bleu (French for "the blue ribbon"), perhaps the most famous name in culinary education, began with L'Ordre des Chevaliers du Saint Esprit, an elite group of French knights that was created in 1578. Members were each presented with the Cross of the Holy Spirit, which hung from a blue ribbon. As the story is often told, the group became famous for its luxurious and extravagant banquets, known, naturally enough, as "cordon bleu."

The dinners ceased when the French Revolution ended the idea of knighthood, but the name lived on, synonymous with fine dining. It eventually became the name of a French culinary magazine, *La Cuisinière Cordon Bleu*, founded in the late nineteenth century. The magazine's success led to it offering cooking lessons provided by some of France's best-known chefs, which led to the establishment of a true cooking school that opened in Paris in 1895.

Le Cordon Bleu quickly established itself among the most elite cooking schools in the world. It closed during the German occupation of Paris in World War II, but reopened after the war, owned and operated by Madame Elisabeth Brassart. Brassart, described by Child in her memoir as "the school's short, thin, rather disagreeable owner,"[7] would become her nemesis throughout her time at the school.

Child arrived at the school at 9:00 A.M. on Tuesday, October 4, 1949, and was disappointed to learn that she had been assigned a beginner's class along with two women who had never cooked before. Not willing to settle, Child marched herself into Madame Brassart's office to plead her case. What she was looking for, she explained, was a far more rigorous program, one that would teach her all the things she had not been able to learn on her own.

For her part, Brassart was unconvinced. She made it quite clear to Child that she did not like her, or, in fact, any Americans. "They can't cook,"[8] she said, right to Child's face. Finally, though, after two days of pleading, Brassart gave in. While she felt that Child did not have the necessary experience to study *haute cuisine* (high-end professional-level cooking), there was a year-long class, geared for "professional restaurateurs," that had just begun that she would be able to place her in. Child agreed, and her formal culinary training began in earnest.

It was clear that the school, still recovering from the effects of the war and its long closing, had seen better days. Dirty pots and pans were everywhere, the kitchens were barely kept clean, and classes often ran short of ingredients. None of that mattered, though. Child loved her teacher, Chef Max Bugnard, a professional chef who had worked under the great Escoffier before opening his own restaurant in Brussels, Belgium. She was eager to learn all that Bugnard, with his years of restaurant experience behind him, had to teach her.

In those days, men ran the world of fine cuisine, so it is not surprising that Child was the only woman in her class. The other 11 students were former American soldiers who were now studying cooking, funded by the GI Bill of Rights, which made higher education affordable for hundreds of thousands of returning veterans. The GIs, most of whom had worked as army cooks during the war, were serious about their cooking and considered their class to be their own private boys' club, so they tried to put Child to the test.

With her great sense of humor and previous experience on mostly male military bases, though, she didn't let them faze her in the least. She wrote in a letter to her family that "it's a free-for-all. Being the only woman, I am being careful to sit back a bit, but am being very cold-blooded indeed in a quiet way (got to be cold-blooded and realistic, but retain appearance of sweetness and gentility)."[9]

Her mornings began at 6:30. She would wake up, dress in the still-dark room so as not to wake Paul, drink a can of tomato juice, and be out the door by 6:50. She would then walk seven blocks to the garage, climb into her car, and drive to school, arriving there well before it opened, which gave her time to visit a cafe, drink a café au lait, and eat warm croissants while reading the day's newspapers.

At 7:20, she would walk to the school and put on her uniform of a white housedress and a blue chef's apron with a clean dish towel tucked neatly into the waist cord. Knives sharpened and ready to go, she would then set to work chopping onions, getting her work station ready for the arrival of Chef Bugnard at 7:30.

Then the cooking would begin, with each student preparing the day's lesson with continuous coaching and instruction from Bugnard. They would be done by 9:30, which gave Child enough time to do some shopping and race home to cook some more, trying her hand at making simple dishes like cheese tarts or *coquilles Saint-Jacques* (a lovely dish of scallops in a creamy sauce). Paul Child would arrive for lunch at 12:30. The couple would talk and catch up on the day's events before Paul returned to work at the embassy and Julia went back to Le Cordon Bleu for afternoon classes.

Demonstration classes were held in the afternoon, which meant that the students would not be cooking. Instead, a visiting chef, with the assistance of two apprentices, would cook and explain three or four dishes—demonstrating, for example, how to prepare a cheese soufflé (*soufflé au fromage*), how to decorate a stuffed boneless chicken, or how to make a dessert such as *charlotte aux pommes* (a classic apple dessert).

These demonstrations, which Child compared to being at a teaching hospital and watching a surgeon perform an operation, lasted until 5:30. She would return home and once again get to work, this time cooking dinner for Paul and, often, for assorted guests, putting into practice what she had just seen prepared in class. "After that one demonstration of Boeuf B, I came home and made the most delicious one I ever ett," she wrote home. "My cooking has always been on the experimental side, these courses will make them SURE."[10] (Boeuf B. is *boeuf bourguignon*, a classic French dish composed of beef slowly braised in red wine until it is so tender you can cut it with a spoon.)

Her schedule made for long, tiring days, but Child thrived on it. At long last, she was learning the secrets behind good cooking. As it turned out, there *were* no secrets. With good teaching, she had what she needed: "a clear, rational guide to making every dish taste the way it should."[11] It was more than just learning how to read a recipe and following it carefully. It was learning how to cook using all of her senses, learning how a dish was supposed to look, smell, and taste, and learning the techniques necessary to do it every

## FRENCH FOOD AND ESCOFFIER

The history of French food goes back as far as the Middle Ages, and the foundation of haute cuisine ("high cuisine") was laid down during the seventeenth century by the chef named La Varenne, who is credited with publishing the first true French cookbook, *Cvisinier francois*. Still, it fell to Georges Auguste Escoffier to modernize haute cuisine and organize what became known as the national cuisine of France.

The influence of Escoffier (1846–1935) is wide-ranging. While working at such famous hotels as the Ritz and the Carlton, he helped to organize the restaurant kitchen as we know it today. Previously, one chef would have been responsible for preparing a dish from start to finish—a time-consuming project. Escoffier divided the kitchen into work stations, a *garde manger* who prepared cold dishes; the *entremettier,* responsible for starches and vegetables; the *rotissieur*, in charge of roasts, grilled, and fried dishes; the *saucier* for sauces and soups; and the *patissier* for all pastries and desserts. By breaking food preparation down into smaller stages (not unlike an assembly line), time was saved, and more elaborate dishes became more widespread.

time. "It is beginning to take effect," she wrote home after just three months at Le Cordon Bleu. "I feel it in my hands, my stomach, my soul."[12]

She was fortunate she had Chef Bugnard to help guide her. He drilled his students in the essentials, in the importance of maintaining the highest standards in cooking. He began with the fundamentals, the building blocks of cooking, teaching his students the classic sauces and the classic techniques, and how to put them together to prepare

Escoffier also had a huge impact on menus and how the meal itself was structured. In his *Livre des menus*, he endorsed what was known as *service à la russe*, defined as serving meals in separate courses on individual plates. (Previously every course was brought out at once, on large, elaborately decorated platters, in the style known as *service à la française*.)

His masterpiece, though, and the book that he is most remembered for, is *Le Guide Culinaire*, first published in 1903, which once and for all laid out the fundamentals of French cooking. In it, Escoffier summed up all that had come before him and then modernized it, creating the style we know today as classic French cooking. All aspects of the dish, including sauces and garnishes, would be used not to mask flavors as they had so often in the past, but simply to make the food taste as it should. With more than 5,000 recipes, *Le Guide Culinaire* is still found and used in restaurants worldwide. It should be no surprise then that Escoffier was known in his lifetime as the king of chefs, and the chef of kings.

great food. And always, he insisted that they analyze as they go. "But how does it *taste*, Madame Scheeld?" was his constant refrain.[13]

Under Bugnard's tutelage, even the simplest dish could become a work of art. In one early class, he asked Child to demonstrate how to prepare *oeufs brouilles* (scrambled eggs). After watching his student firmly whip eggs and cream them together until they were frothy before pouring them into a very hot frying pan with butter, he could only react in horror. "That is absolutely wrong!"[14] He proceeded to demonstrate the *right* way.

Chef Bugnard cracked two eggs into a bowl, added a little salt and pepper, and then gently blended the yolks and whites together. "Like *this*," he said. "Not too much."[15] He smeared the bottom and sides of a frying pan with butter before gently pouring in the eggs. The next step was to put the pan over low heat. At first, nothing happened. But then, after three minutes, the eggs began to thicken up like a custard. Only then did he go to work, stirring the eggs, pulling the pan on and off the heat, pulling the egg curds together. "Keep them a little bit loose; this is very important," he noted, "*Now* the cream or butter," he told her, adding, "This will stop the cooking, you see?" before turning the beautifully scrambled eggs onto a plate, garnishing with parsley, and saying, "*Voila!*"[16]

The eggs were perfect, as you would expect. And even though it was a dish Bugnard must have prepared thousands of times, he made it with the same pride and pleasure as he always did. Bugnard drilled into his students that they should *always* pay attention, *learn* the proper technique, and, perhaps most importantly, enjoy their own cooking.

For Julia Child, it was, as she said in her memoir, a remarkable lesson. No dish, even the humblest scrambled egg, was too much trouble for him—any dish, no matter how simple, should get the same care and dedication. "You never forget a beautiful thing that you have made," he said. "Even after you eat it, it stays with you—always."[17]

Her time at Le Cordon Bleu woke something deep within her. Her whole life, it seemed, she had been happy to live "a butterfly life of fun, with hardly a care in the world"[18] Never before had she taken something seriously; but at cooking school, as she said:

> I suddenly discovered that cooking was a rich and layered and endlessly fascinating subject. The best way to describe it is to say that I fell in love with French food—the tastes, the processes, the history, the endless variations, the rigorous discipline, the creativity, the wonderful people, the equipment, the rituals.[19]

There were still mistakes in her cooking, including one memorable meal of eggs Florentine (a variation on eggs benedict, with poached eggs sitting on top of an English muffin and creamed spinach, the whole dish topped with a luscious hollandaise sauce) that she claimed was "the most VILE eggs Florentine I have ever imagined could be made outside of England."[20] But now, after her training, she had learned enough to know where she had made her mistake and how to fix it the next time. Perhaps most importantly, she learned never to apologize to her guests. Grin and bear it, and then move on, knowing you'll do better the next time.

## MOVING ON

Child realized that she was beginning to outgrow her classes at Le Cordon Bleu—her skills had progressed far beyond those of her classmates. "After 6 months they don't know the proportions for a béchamel or how to clean a chicken the French way."[21] She dropped out of school but hired Chef Bugnard to give her private lessons for another six months.

Elisabeth Brassart, the owner of the cooking school Le Cordon Bleu, is shown giving a student her diploma in 1950. Julia Child had a much harder time receiving her recognition from Brassart, who was a thorn in Child's side during her studies at Le Cordon Bleu. Eventually, Child did get a certificate of completion.

With one year of training behind her, she decided she was ready to take the final exam and receive an official diploma from Le Cordon Bleu. There was one problem, though: Standing in her way was her longtime nemesis Madame Brassart, the school's strict director who had always disliked Child for thinking that she was too good to take the amateur course, for forcing her way into the professional course, and then dropping out before even completing it.

Now, this tall American woman had the gall to ask for her diploma. At first, Madame Brassart refused to even allow her to take the test. After months of pressure, however, including a letter from Child hinting ever so subtly that the American embassy was wondering why she was being treated so badly, Brassart gave in.

She did, however, get her revenge. She gave Child the beginner's exam, the same exam that was given to housewives taking the six-week course that she had fled from more than a year earlier. Child nearly failed the test. She easily passed the written section, describing, for example, how to prepare a brown stock, the best way to cook green vegetables, and how to make the wonderfully rich concoction of clarified butter, eggs, and tarragon that is sauce béarnaise.

But when it came to the cooking portion of the exam, Child, to put it politely, choked. While making a dish that was supposed to use a soft-boiled egg, she substituted one that was poached. She put too much milk into the caramel custard and forgot what went into an *côtelettes de veau en surprise* (veal, mushrooms, and ham, cooked, then reheated and served in a paper bag). It was, not surprisingly, a frustrating experience.

It was a simple question of emphasis. Child had spent so much time studying the more complicated aspects of French cooking that she had "neglected to look at the primary things."[22] Besides, as she often said, it did not bother her to forget what went into the paper-bag dish anyway—it was a silly dish made only by housewives trying to impress the boss's wife.

Eventually Madame gave in and presented Child not with an official diploma, but with a certificate of completion. Child never forgave Brassard, including her for years on the very short list of people whom she absolutely hated. When the time came for her to teach cooking, she vowed, she would train her students "through friendliness and encouragement and professionalism"[23] and not in the manner of Madame Brassart. Besides, as Child never tired of pointing out, Madame Brassart wasn't even French—she was Belgian.

## FINDING HER PARTNER

At the same time that Child was studying and attempting to graduate from Le Cordon Bleu, a friend introduced her to a woman who was just as food-crazy as Child. Her name was Simone Beck Fischbacher—known to friends as "Simca." If Paul Child was Julia's ideal life partner, Beck would become her ideal work partner. She was, as Laura Shapiro pointed out, Child's "first culinary soul mate"[24] and a woman whose lifetime of experience preparing French home cooking was the perfect balance to Child's classroom education.

Beck's mind contained a treasure trove of classic French recipes and techniques. Everything the largely self-taught Beck tasted served to inspire even more recipes—Child often said that Beck threw off ideas like a fountain. They were the perfect couple, two women in love with food, France, and life, whose lives meshed professionally and personally. As Shapiro noted in her biography of Child, "As soon as they were introduced, the two women started talking about French food and didn't let up until Simca's death forty years later."[25]

Still, the two ran into walls despite their obvious love and respect for French food. In France in the 1950s, men ruled the world of haute cuisine. Women did not wait tables at the best restaurants, did not cook in the best restaurants, and were barred from belonging to the elite dining clubs where male gourmands met to talk about and eat the finest food prepared by France's best (male) chefs.

There was just one place where women like Julia Child and Simone Beck could meet with other gourmands. It was Le Cercle des Gourmettes, a club run by female gourmands. The club met for lunch on a regular basis, and the meals served at those lunches remained some of Child's longest-lasting food memories, as she once said that they marked "the real beginning of French gastronomical life for me."[26] She continued:

> I soon realized I had never really lived before. There was always an elegant first course, such as fresh artichoke bottoms stuffed with sweetbreads and served with a truffled béarnaise, or a most elaborately poached fish garnished with mushroom duxelles and lobster tails, and sauced with a creamy puree of crab. The main course might be boned duck, or game in season. Then came dessert, a sorbet aux poires, garnished with pears poached in wine and served in a meringue nut-shell, or a fancy mousse.[27]

For Julia Child, it was an amazing experience. All the fine cuisine she had read about, studied, and learned to prepare was there before her, in all its delicious glory. Add to that the delight she felt in being with other women equally interested in cooking in all its variety, and she was in food heaven.

Among the women she met there was another friend of Beck's, Louisette Bertholle. The three hit it off well and came up with the idea of opening a cooking school of their own, aimed at teaching Americans either traveling or living in Paris how to cook. The school, which would ultimately be called L'Ecole des Trois Gourmandes, opened in January 1952, with classes held in Julia Child's kitchen.

## THE SCHOOL OF THE THREE HAPPY EATERS

It was designed to be the opposite of Child's experience at Le Cordon Bleu—small, informal classes, with the emphasis on French cooking (naturally) and classical technique. By focusing on technique, the basic kitchen skills that every chef needs to know, the students would have the tools necessary to cook any *other* cuisine. Child clearly laid out their goals:

> Our aim is to teach you how to cook. We are prepared to show the basic methods of French cooking, which, when you have mastered them, should enable you to follow a recipe, or invent any "little dish" that you want. We feel that when one has learned to use one's tools quickly and efficiently one can then provide one's own short-cuts. . . . The recipes we give you are basic recipes, with practically no frills. We want them to be as clear and complete as possible. And we want you to feel, after we have done something in class, that you really have understood all about doing it.[28]

Even though Child was beginning a career of teaching people to cook, the basic elements were in place—the importance on learning the fundamentals of cooking and the emphasis on precision and clarity in recipes so that students could gain the self-confidence to repeat what they learned in Julia's kitchen and to use what they learned to explore cooking on their own.

An extraordinary attention to detail not only went into devising the recipes used in class, but into the lesson plans as well, with "Prof. Julia," "Prof. Simca," and "Prof. Louisette" given precise instructions as to what each was supposed to do and when to do it. On the lesson plan for March 12, 1952, for example, the menu included *blanquette*

With Simone Beck and Louisette Bertholle, Julia Child opened L'Ecole des Trois Gourmandes, a cooking school, in 1952 in Paris. With small, informal classes, the school aimed to teach Americans how to cook French cuisine. Here, Child is shown in the kitchen where classes were held.

*de veau*, a creamy veal stew; plain rice and risotto, a more complicated Italian rice dish; a salad; and two dessert tarts, banana and mixed fruit.

Prof. Julia gave the introduction, then worked on the *blanquette*, which took the longest to prepare: She taught the students how to prepare the meat, the shallots, and the parsley. Prof. Simca handled the onions and mushrooms. (Prof. Louisette, facing a series of personal problems, was not there that day.)

Moving on to the other courses, Prof. Simca led the students in the preparation of the *crème patissiere* or pastry cream. Prof. Julia handled the salad and the *veloute* sauce for the veal. To finish off, it fell to Prof. Simca to teach the students how to carefully thicken their sauce by using a liaison, a mixture of cream and egg yolks.

## A PROPOSAL

While some of the recipes used at L'Ecole des Trois Gour-mandes came from many hours spent by Child and Beck in perfecting their recipes, others came directly from Beck and Bertholle. For years, the two longtime friends had been working on a French cookbook aimed at Americans, written in English and to be published in America.

Bertholle was half-American, and on one of her trips to the United States, she had offered the manuscript to Sumner Putnam, the head of the small publishing company Ives Washburn. Putnam was interested in the manuscript but had no experience in marketing and selling cookbooks. In addition, by Bertholle and Beck's own admission, the manuscript was not in very good shape, having originally been written in French and then translated into rough English.

To test the market, Putnam hired his own translator, cookbook author Helmut Ripperger, and asked him to come up with a kind of "teaser" for the book, a highly abbrevi-ated collection of recipes from the manuscript to be titled "What's Cooking in France." Beck and Bertholle agreed to go along with the project. When they received the finished copy, however, they were dismayed by the number of errors it contained. Not knowing what to do next, but not willing to give up on the project, they turned for help to their American friend, the woman who loved French cooking as much as they did—Julia Child.

In August 1952, they asked Child if she might be interested in helping them finish their book. The answer was quick and certain—of course she would. This was the kind of project she had long wanted to do, to help introduce and teach the French cooking she loved to American housewives back home who were, she was certain, eager to learn how to prepare the best foods possible.

When she looked over the manuscript, though, she discovered that she was going to need to do more than just translate it into English. Unwilling to take any recipe at face value, she went into her kitchen to test a few, just as they were written, to find out if they worked *and* if they were workable for an American housewife.

To her surprise, the recipes were largely unusable. Some were too short, making assumptions that the reader would know how to do something that, in all likelihood, they did not know how to do. Other recipes went on too long and were too complicated, with instructions that were too vague for a novice cook.

There was, she told her partners, nothing in the manuscript worth saving. By the end of November, the three women had come up with a plan for an entirely new book. Child, who had taken over the lead position in the project, wrote to Putnam to explain exactly what they wanted to do.

Instead of just another cookbook, they would write a teaching manual, built around a series of basic themes and variations. It would be written in a voice that didn't speak down to the reader but spoke directly to them. She went on to acknowledge that yes, there were other French cookbooks on the market, but theirs would be unique. It would be logical, making clear to the reader exactly "why" one did something, while also explaining how things could go wrong, and, most importantly, how to fix them when they did.

It would be a mammoth undertaking. They were proposing to write a completely new book that would not only explain the technical aspects of French cooking but also explore the entire range of French cooking, from simple farmhouse fare to the classic haute cuisine served at the very best restaurants. Child was convinced, though, that it could be done, and done quickly.

She promised Putnam that she would have a newly revised chapter on sauces completed shortly and that the entire manuscript would be on his desk within six months. Little did she dream that the predicted months would quickly turn to years and that the manuscript would sit on the desk of several publishers before finally finding a home.

# Mastering the Art of French Cooking

Once Julia Child decided to get on board with the cookbook, she was there all the way. By writing the book, she would fulfill her early dream of being a writer, while at the same time establish herself as a culinary authority *and* make fine cooking available to American households. It was, for her, the perfect project.

She set to work with all the methodical determination she had demonstrated since discovering her passion for cooking. Each recipe was checked, tested, and checked again. When working on soups, for example, each day at the Child household meant a different soup. Take the example of just one soup, *soupe aux choux*—a simple cabbage soup. She would begin by looking at Simca Beck's original recipe, as well as other authoritative recipes for cabbage soup from a number of noted French chefs and writers.

Child would read them all and then make the soup three ways—two times following recipes exactly as written, then a third time, adapting the recipe for a pressure cooker, a popular time-saving device of the time. At dinner, it would fall to Paul Child to be her guinea pig. Even when he complimented all three soups, it wasn't enough for her. She knew there was a way to make them taste even better, if only she could discover it.

Should the cabbage be blanched (lightly boiled) before being used in the broth? Maybe a different *kind* of cabbage would do the trick? Maybe the cabbage needed to be cooked for less time in the broth? Maybe less time in the pressure cooker would make it taste better? The lesson she had learned from Chef Bugnard and his scrambled eggs still held true. Even for a dish as simple and basic as cabbage soup, there was no compromise. As she wrote in her memoir, *My Life in France*:

> I had to iron out all of these questions of how and why and for what reason; otherwise, we'd end up with just an ordinary recipe—which was not the point of the book. I felt we should strive to show our readers how to make everything top-notch and explain, if possible, why things work one way but not another. There would be no compromise![1]

She would never compromise on her goal: to teach American housewives (it was assumed then that anybody cooking at home would be a housewife) that there is something about French food that makes it unique. The goal of the French chef, whether making the simplest farmhouse roast chicken or the finest of elaborate haute cuisine dishes, was purely to make food taste as it should. Child knew full well the struggle she had had to master cooking. Simple cookbooks weren't enough—it had been good teaching that set her free. This was what she hoped the book, now titled *French Home Cooking*, would do for others.

# LA BONNE CUISINE

Julia Child often said that *La Bonne Cuisine*, first published in 1927, was her favorite French cookbook. Little is known about Madame Saint-Ange or where she gained the culinary background that allowed her to move easily from restaurant haute cuisine to the simplest family fare. But, as with *Mastering the Art of French Cooking*, in *La Bonne Cuisine*, Madame Saint-Ange, in a calm and cheerful voice, takes the reader through nearly 1,300 recipes, along with the fundamental techniques needed to make those dishes.

It is hard to determine exactly how much *Mastering the Art of French Cooking* owed to Madame Saint-Ange, but the influence is considerable. Take, for example, Saint-Ange's instructions for scrambled eggs. She discusses the proper pan, describes various ways of beating the eggs including the pros and cons of using a whisk versus a wooden spoon, specifies the shape of the wooden spoon one *should* use if that turned out to be the tool of choice, then moved to instructions on how to cook the eggs, with notes on how to avoid problems and what to do if things go wrong anyway.

At the very least, *Le Bonne Cuisine* showed Child that a cookbook could be more than just a collection of recipes; it could be a teaching tool as well. It is little wonder that Child in 1987 described it as a "book that I adore and that was my mentor in my early days in France. . . . It was a carefully thought-out, very personal book. . . . I still love it."*

---

* Madame E. Saint-Ange, *La Bonne Cuisine*. Berkeley, Calif.: Ten Speed Press, 2005.

One year into the project, Child received a letter from Sumner Putnam, the head of the Ives Washburn publishing company. He noted that the book was going to be a huge volume and worried that it might not appeal to the American woman, who, he was concerned, wanted only a book that would give her cooking "the French touch,"[2] while adding that "if the recipe . . . can't be easily used by the stupidest pupil in your school, then it is too complicated."[3]

Obviously, the letter caused concern among the three authors. Child, in particular, was worried that, even though Putnam seemed serious about publishing their book, his company was not very well respected. Was it really the right publisher for them? After all, they had no legal contract with him and had received no money. On top of that, he wanted to receive a finished manuscript by March 1, 1953, just months away.

Child was ready to pull out and find another publisher, but Beck and Bertholle convinced her that they should stay the course, since they were all unknown authors and had a publisher willing to publish their book. Child reluctantly agreed, and on behalf of her fellow authors, wrote a letter to Putnam explaining, once again, exactly what they aimed to do.

It would *not* be just another cookbook. Instead, it would be an introduction, a classroom in the methods of French cooking *plus* recipes. The book, while written in "an informal and humane tone that would make cooking approachable and fun,"[4] would at the same time be a serious reference work. The trio would be doing something never before attempted—breaking down the seemingly complex rules of French cooking into a series of logical steps that anyone could follow. As she continued in her letter:

> It is not enough that the "how" [of making hollandaise or mayonnaise] be explained. One should know the "why," the pitfalls, the remedies, the keeping,

the serving, etc. This is a new type of cookbook. Competition in this field is stiff, but we feel that this may well be a major work on French cooking . . . and could continue to sell for years.[5]

Putnam never responded to her letter. He never responded to her extensively researched chapter on sauces. Fortunately, Child had also sent three top-secret sauce recipes (hollandaise, mayonnaise, and *beurre blanc*—a rich white butter sauce) to four friends to test in American kitchens using American ingredients. (French ingredients, like butter, can be very different from their American versions.)

One of those friends, Avis De Voto, was the wife of the well-known American writer Bernard De Voto. She loved what she read of Child's work, thought the book had real potential, and asked permission to send the chapter to her husband's publisher, Houghton Mifflin. Fed up with the lack of communication with Sumner Putnam, permission was granted. Now, all they could do was keep working and wait to hear what Houghton Mifflin, a well-respected publisher, had to say.

Six weeks later, Child received word from Avis De Voto that Houghton Mifflin's managing editor, Dorothy de Santillana, was "tickled pink"[6] with what she had read. An offer soon followed, including what was then a sizable advance of $750. The contract with Houghton Mifflin was signed, a letter was sent to Putnam informing him of their decision, and as Child wrote to Avis De Voto, the realization hit her "with awesome seriousness that the real work is about to begin."[7]

Julia Child, Simone Beck, and Louisette Bertholle were convinced that the manuscript could be completed within one year. Little did they know that it would be six years and that Julia and Paul Child would move five times before their book would hit bookstores.

## WRITING AND MOVING

Much to their dismay, in 1954, Paul Child's assignment changed. No longer would he be based in Paris. Instead, he was reassigned to Marseilles, a Mediterranean port city on the southern coast of France. Julia had no other option but to pack up their belongings, including the pounds of manuscript already written, say good-bye to her friends and colleagues, and leave Paris, the city she had grown to love.

It was the first of several moves. From Marseilles the couple moved to Bonn, Germany, then to Washington, D.C., then to Oslo, Norway, before Paul finally retired back to the United States in 1961. Throughout this period, Child was rarely able to sit down, face to face, to work with Beck and was forced to rely on the mail to carry on their collaboration. (Bertholle's role diminished throughout this period before she dropped out of the project entirely, although she still received credit for the book.)

Recipes, suggestions, revisions, and notes all flew back and forth between Beck in Paris and Child wherever she happened to be living at the time. Sometimes the two agreed. Sometimes they did not. The battle over the recipe for cassoulet, the legendary French dish (a simple peasant dish really) of beans slowly baked with various cuts of meat, raged on and on for weeks.

It all came down to a simple question. Was there one "true" version of the dish, or were there as many versions as there were cooks preparing them, each with something to offer? In her usual thorough manner, Child set out to research every possible variation of the dish, each in its own way classic, and each very "French," ultimately producing a pile of papers over two inches (five centimeters) thick.

For Beck, however, there was only one way to make cassoulet. War between Child and Beck raged over one ingredient: *confit d'oie*. "Confit" is a classic cooking term

The recipe for the classic bean dish cassoulet caused a bit of contention between Julia Child and Simone Beck as they were writing their book. Beck insisted that the only true recipe for cassoulet was made with confit of goose, as pictured here. Child argued that other meats could be used.

that in this case describes goose legs—the *d'oie*—that have been slowly cooked in their own fat and are preserved by storing them completely submerged in that fat.

Beck insisted that without the confit of goose, it wasn't a cassoulet. Child reminded her that they were writing for Americans, most of whom had never even heard of *confit d'oie*, and, in any event, would find it next to impossible to buy. (That may have been true then. But with the explosion of gourmet markets brought about in no small part by Child, the ingredient is much more readily available today.)

Child reminded her friend that, while they wanted their instructions to be as accurate as possible, all that accuracy would be for naught if the person using the recipe could not buy the necessary ingredients. "The important item is flavor," Child wrote to Beck, "which comes largely from the liquid the beans and meats are cooked in,"[8] before pointing out to her one respected source after another that did not include preserved goose.

Finally, a compromise of sorts was reached. There would be one "master recipe" for cassoulet using pork or

## IN HER OWN WORDS

Julia Child on the need for a hearty appetite to eat one of her favorite bean dishes:

> Cassoulet, that best of bean feasts, is everyday fare for a peasant but ambrosia for a gastronome, though its ideal consumer is a 300-pound (136-kilogram) blocking back who has been splitting firewood nonstop for the last twelve hours on a subzero day in Manitoba.*

* Steve Meyer and Dayton Azevedo, "Cassoulet," 5 stars in your kitchen's Blog, August 25, 2010, http://5starsinyourkitchen. wordpress.com/2010/08/25/cassoulet-goes-to-italy.

lamb and homemade sausage. Following that would be four variations on the basic recipe, including one using *confit d'oie*. Included along with the recipe was an explanation of the dish, menu suggestions, an in-depth look at the kinds of dried beans that could be used, as well as a list showing the aspiring cook how to break the recipe down into workable stages.

All in all, six pages are devoted to cassoulet. It may seem like too much information. But for an aspiring chef who wants to make the dish, all of that information and advice provides the confidence that a great dish is virtually guaranteed by following the recipe and using Child's techniques.

If that one essentially simple dish took so long to work into a basic recipe, it is easy to imagine why the book took so long to write. There were so many questions to answer, so many recipes to refine, and so many techniques to be broken down and made simple to explain.

And, once Child returned to the States, there were so many American ingredients that had to be tested. Much to her dismay, what she found was that American supermarkets were full of products labeled as "gourmet" but that were anything but. As she wrote:

> Instant cake mixes, TV dinners, frozen vegetables, canned mushrooms, fish sticks, Jell-O salads, marshmallows, spray-can whipped cream, and other horrible glop. This gave me pause. Would there be a place in the U.S.A. for a book like ours? Were we hopelessly out of step with the times?[9]

It was as far as one could get from the kind of food she wanted Americans to be cooking and eating—food made with fresh ingredients, food made for the love of cooking and serving good food, not just food slapped on the table because it was fast and convenient. The question of whether Americans could be encouraged to prepare food that was not fast and convenient was still an unanswered question.

## WILL IT BE PUBLISHED?

The early indicators did not look good. By the end of 1957, with the completed manuscript in sight, Child and Beck tried to publish a few articles in American magazines, featuring recipes from their book. There were no takers. An article featuring a recipe for the Belgian dish *waterzooi de poulet*, a rather simple poached chicken with a rich creamy sauce, was rejected by *McCall's*, when food editor Helen McCully wrote that if she showed it to her editor "she would probably faint dead away," adding that "to the non-cook it certainly looks like a chore."[10]

Child tried again, with a recipe for a boned stuffed duck baked in a pastry crust. She pointed out to McCully that, while the dish might seem impossible for anyone other than a trained chef to make, it was easy enough for even a beginning cook "if supplied with good directions such as ours."[11] Again, no luck.

With that, Child began to worry that maybe she had been mistaken, maybe she was completely out of step with the times and all her hard work had been for nothing. She had little time to worry, though, because the due date for delivery of the final manuscript to Houghton Mifflin was coming up and it was still nowhere near completion.

Once it was finally finished, Child and Beck delivered the manuscript to Dorothy de Santillana in person. The manuscript, more than 800 pages of incredibly detailed recipes covering only sauces and poultry, was rejected outright. It was just too much, de Santillana told them, stating simply that "this is not the book we contracted for."[12] She still had faith in Child and Beck, though, and gave them an opportunity to rethink and redesign their manuscript.

Frozen foods and other convenience foods were popular in the United States in the late 1950s. As Julia Child and Simone Beck were completing their manuscript, Child began to wonder if they had overestimated the audience for their book. Could Americans be encouraged to prepare meals that were not quick and easy?

The pair decided to abandon their encyclopedic approach to French cooking, and, as they wrote to de Santillana, "proposed to prepare you a short and snappy book directed to the somewhat sophisticated housewife-chauffeur."[13] The book would be only around 300 pages, and along with authentic recipes, it would include hints on how to jazz up frozen and canned products. It was exactly the kind of book and the kind of thinking about cooking that Child hated.

After just a few weeks of work, she realized that she just could not do it. Child could not put her name on a cookbook that showed harried housewives how to make sauces from canned soups, how to make casseroles from frozen vegetables, and placed speed and convenience over flavor. If her original manuscript was too detailed for an American audience and the new proposal was too "dumbed-down" to satisfy Child and Beck, they would have to find a middle ground.

The new proposal found that ground. "This is to be a collection of good French dishes of the simpler sort, directed frankly to those who enjoy cooking and have a feeling for food."[14] The emphasis would be less *haute cuisine* and more *cuisine bourgeoisie* ("middle-class cooking"). The challenge, as Child now saw it, would be to bridge the cultural divide between France and the United States, and to do so by not only emphasizing the basic rules, the building blocks of cooking, but also by stressing the importance of "including *fun* and *love* in the preparation of a meal!"[15]

On September 1, 1959, the revised manuscript, 750 pages long and entitled *French Recipes for American Cooks*, was complete. After being given to a friend to type up, it was sent to Houghton Mifflin. It had been seven years since Child had started working on the book. It was time, she thought, for all her hard work to pay off and for the book to be published at long last.

# The Publication
# of a Classic

It had taken a year and a half of rewriting and revising, but by September 1959, Julia Child and Simone Beck had a manuscript ready to be sent to Dorothy de Santillana at Houghton Mifflin. After poring over the book for four days, she gave the eager authors her verdict: "I surely do not know of any other compendium so amazingly, startlingly accurate or so inclusive."[1] The manuscript still had to get final approval from the company's executives, but finally, it looked as if Child's dream work had found a home.

Two months later, though, Child received a letter from Houghton Mifflin's editor-in-chief, Paul Brooks. It took her some time to gather up the nerve to open and read the letter, but when she did, she learned that the company had decided not to publish her book. Brooks praised the manuscript, calling it "a work of culinary science as much as of culinary art,"[2] but, he said, at 750 pages, it would simply be too expensive to produce and require too heavy an investment from his company with little hope of making a profit. He added that:

> After the first project grew to encyclopedic size you agreed with us that the book . . . was to be a much smaller, simpler book. . . . You . . . spoke of the revised project as a "short simple book directed to the housewife chauffeur." The present book could never be called this. It is a big, expensive cookbook of elaborate information and might well prove formidable to the American housewife. She might easily clip one of these recipes out of a magazine but be frightened by the book as a whole.
>
> I am aware that this reaction will be a disappointment and . . . I suggest that you try the book immediately on some other publisher.[3]

Child later received a letter from de Santillana, who explained the reason behind the reason that the manuscript was turned down. It was men who rejected the manuscript, certain that the book was too challenging for the female home cook, who would rather, they were sure, use a cookbook that presented them with shortcuts to something *like* French cooking rather than a book on how to prepare the real thing.

It was a disheartening decision. Was Houghton Mifflin right? Was the book too intimidating, too complicated, too *much* for the housewife who just wanted to get a hot meal on the table with as little fuss and muss as possible? Was a simplified version of a French classic the way to go?

Take *coq au vin* for example, the classic dish of chicken braised with red wine, bacon, onions, and mushrooms. In a popular cookbook of the time, the recipe for the dish instructed the reader to: "Cut up two broilers. Brown them in butter with bacon, sliced onions, and sliced mushrooms. Cover with red wine and bake for two hours."[4] Simple enough, and you would probably get an adequate dish out of it. For the aspiring chef, though, much was left unanswered. How do you cut up a chicken into parts? How much butter should you use? How much bacon, onions, and mushrooms? What kind of mushrooms? How brown is brown? So many questions left unanswered.

In Child's recipe for *coq au vin*, she carefully takes the aspiring cook through two pages of instructions, explaining each step of the cooking process—a process guaranteed to turn out an outstanding dish. With Child's recipe and instruction, an additional 10 to 15 minutes of work and attention to detail reward the chef with a dish she can be proud of, a dish that is true to the traditions of French cuisine.

The question that remained was this: Was anybody interested in taking the time to prepare good food? After the rejection by Houghton Mifflin, Child's confidence in the project was fairly well shaken. Maybe, she thought, it was time to give up on the idea.

Her good friend Avis De Voto would have none of it. Without discussing it with either Child or Beck, she sent the manuscript to an old friend, Bill Koshland, an executive at Alfred A. Knopf, one of the most respected publishing companies in the country. Koshland, an amateur food expert, had heard about Child's manuscript through the publishing grapevine.

He was convinced that there was a market for the book; that along with the explosion of interest in fast, convenient processed foods, another market was also developing. There was an audience out there, he thought, of people who had traveled, people who were subscribing to magazines like

In 2001, Julia Child and her book editor, Judith Jones, spoke at a fund-raiser for a library in St. Johnsbury, Vermont. Jones, an editor at Alfred A. Knopf, pushed for the publication of *Mastering the Art of French Cooking* and came up with the book's title.

*Gourmet*, people who were rejecting the frozen food culture and wanted something more. Those were the people, he was certain, who were eager for a book such as Child's to appear.

The publisher Alfred A. Knopf, on the other hand, had his doubts. The company had recently published *Classic French Cooking*, and Knopf was certain that another French cookbook was not needed. To placate Koshland, though, he passed the manuscript on to a young editor named Judith Jones. It was the luckiest break Julia Child could have had.

Jones, a talented cook who, like Child, had developed a passion for French cooking while living in Paris, understood immediately what the book was trying to do. Together with her husband, editor Evan Jones, she tested recipe after recipe in her home kitchen, turning out perfect *boeuf bourguignon* to serve at a dinner party, trying Child's "secret" methods for perfect sauces, and flipping omelets until she was convinced that the book was something that she *had* to publish. Now all she and Koshland had to do was persuade Knopf and his wife, Blanche, to feel the same way.

In mid-1960, Julia and Paul Child were still living in Oslo, Norway, when she received a letter from Judith Jones. After years of disappointment, Child was prepared for the worst, and she took a deep breath before opening Jones's letter.

> We have come to the conclusion that it is a unique book that we would be very proud to have on the Knopf list. . . . I have been authorized to make you an offer. . . . We consider it the best and only working French cookbook to date which will do for French cooking here in America what Rombauer's *The Joy of Cooking* once did for standard cooking, and we will sell it that way. . . . It is certainly a beautifully organized, clearly written, wonderfully instructive manuscript. You have already revolutionized my own efforts in the cuisine and everyone I have let sample a recipe or talked to about the book is already pledged not to buy another cookbook.[5]

It was all she could have hoped for and more. Knopf offered the authors an advance of $1,500 to be paid out against future royalties. The price of the book would be around $10, and it would come out in the fall of 1961, just in time for the holidays. To simplify matters, the contract would be with Child alone, who would then work out the financial arrangements with Beck and Bertholle.

There was one immediate and major change. Jones hated the book's working title, *French Recipes for American Cooks*, which she felt did not do the book's scope justice. Child was stumped and threw a contest among her friends to come up with a short, catchy book title. Various titles were suggested: *Le Bonne Cuisine Francaise*; *The Noble Art of French Cooking*; *The Witchcraft of French Cooking*; *How, Why, What to Cook in the French Way*. None of them seemed right. None of them gave the reader the sense that Child's book was *the* book on French cooking, the only one they would ever need.

It fell to Judith Jones to come up with the winner. Working from her office in New York, she played with a list of words, mixing and matching them, trying to come up with just the right combination that would suggest the book's range, its emphasis on the fundamentals, and its focus on French cooking.

She started with *The Master French Cookbook* before moving on to *The French Cooking Master*, *The Mastery of French Cooking*, and *How to Master French Cooking*. These were close, but not quite there yet. Then, on November 18, 1960, Jones wrote to Child informing her that she had finally found the right title: *Mastering the Art of French Cooking*. Child loved the use of the active verb "mastering," and agreed to it immediately, and, after some persuasion, Beck agreed to it as well. The only person who had any doubts, it seemed, was Alfred A. Knopf himself, who said, "I'll eat my hat if anyone buys a book with that title!"[6] It would be up to the team of Jones, Child, and Beck to prove him wrong.

## MANY CHANGES ALL AT ONCE

Over the next year, Child's life would change more than she could possibly have imagined. Paul Child reached the decision that, after 18 years in the Foreign Service, it was time for him to retire. On May 19, 1961, he left government service, and the couple prepared to return home to the United States.

Their time was spent doing more than just packing and saying good-bye to friends. Julia had received the galleys, the final copies for her review before the book would be printed and published, all 15 pounds (7 kilograms) worth. She discovered that proofreading was hard work: There were mistakes to be fixed (originally writing ¼ cup of almond extract, let's say, when she meant to write ¼ teaspoon); there were things that she had forgotten to write (such as covering a pot before it went into the oven); and there were occasional heated arguments with Beck about what should be included in the published book.

Finally, though, the big date arrived. In late September 1961, while settling into her new home in Cambridge, Massachusetts, Child was able to hold in her hands the bound copy of *Mastering the Art of French Cooking* by Beck, Bertholle, and Child. The book's official publication date was set for October 16, and Beck was going to fly over from Paris for the big event. All that was left to do was wait for the unveiling of the book and see what the reaction of critics would be.

## THE REACTION

Two days after publication, Craig Claiborne of the *New York Times* wrote the first of the many glowing reviews the book received.

> What is probably the most comprehensive, laudable and monumental work on [French cooking] was published this week. . . . It will probably remain as the definitive work for nonprofessionals. This is not a book for those with a superficial interest in

In this August 1992 photograph, Julia Child showed off some tomatoes in the kitchen of her home in Cambridge, Massachusetts. In 1961, just as *Mastering the Art of French Cooking* was being published, the Childs moved to the Cambridge home, after Paul Child had left the Foreign Service.

food. But for those who take fundamental delight in the pleasures of cuisine, "Mastering the Art of French Cooking" may well become a vade mecum [a handbook] in the kitchen. It is written in the simplest terms possible and without compromise or condescension. The recipes are glorious, whether they are for a simple egg in aspic or a fish soufflé. At a glance it is conservatively estimated that there are a thousand or more recipes in the book. All are painstakingly edited and written as if each were a masterpiece, and most of them are.[7]

As Julia Child noted, she and Beck could not have written a better review themselves.

Sales upon first publication were slow but steady. In the fall of 1962, the Book-of-the-Month Club made *Mastering the Art of French Cooking* a dividend selection, with the hope of possibly distributing around 12,000 copies. By March, nearly 65,000 books had been shipped with orders still coming in, and the book became the most popular dividend in the club's long history.

Indeed, by 1974, the *New York Times* placed the book on its list of the century's best-selling cookbooks, with nearly 1.5 million copies sold. The book had succeeded beyond Child's wildest expectations. The audience that Child was sure existed, the one that was tired of fast but tasteless convenience foods and eager to learn how to create fine cuisine in their own homes, snatched up copies of her book and made them their culinary bibles. There was an audience, much larger than expected, who were interested in cooking serious food, who took their food seriously.

Late in 1961, Child wrote a letter to Beck, trying to put into words her feelings about what separated French cooking from that of other nations. She boiled it down to four basic ideas:

## DID YOU KNOW?

Although you might think that Julia Child spent her time eating only the finest gourmet foods, she did have more commonplace favorites. In fact, she once sent shockwaves through the culinary community by confessing her fondness for McDonald's french fries! Interestingly enough, when McDonald's changed the fat it cooked its fries in from beef tallow to a more healthy fat, she complained that the quality had gone down.

Craig Claiborne, shown in his kitchen in 1990, was the food critic for the *New York Times* from 1959 to 1987. He wrote a glowing review of *Mastering the Art of French Cooking*, saying that "the recipes are glorious."

Serious interest in food and its preparation. Tradition of good cooking . . . which forms French tastes from youth. Enjoyment of cooking for its own sake— LOVE. Willingness to take the few extra minutes to be sure things are done as they should be done.[8]

You'll note that except for "French tastes," there is nothing on the list that could not be said about any other cuisine. Instead, what the list does is present in a nutshell Child's general outlook on food, even with her devotion to all things French. What mattered to Child, the highest praise she could give, was that the cook was "serious."

Serious cooks, according to Child, were people who were careful about what they cooked and knowledgeable about what they were doing, and whose pleasure in cooking was evident in their food. Those who were not interested in devoting a few extra minutes to their cooking, who did not actually *care* about what they were doing, would never be serious cooks.

Child's constant refrain was simple: "We are aiming at PEOPLE WHO LIKE TO COOK."[9] According to her, even the most basic supermarket ingredients could, when cooked with love and patience, be turned into authentic and delicious French dishes. And thanks to *Mastering the Art of French Cooking*, readers around the country were learning that they, too, could cook fine food.

Reading about it, though, was one thing. Some people needed further proof. A little more than a year after the book's publication, Child would begin to appear on television in houses across the country *showing* viewers just how, with the right techniques, anybody could do it. In the process, she would change the face of American cooking and become one of America's most beloved television personalities. She would become, in the eyes of the nation, the French Chef.

# America Falls in Love with Julia

As previously mentioned, the pilot episodes for Julia Child's show were taped by WGBH in the summer of 1962. They aired soon after, and while the programs themselves have been lost, the surviving letters that poured into the station show that, even at that early stage, Child had a strong instinct on how to use television to her best advantage. One letter stated:

> I loved the way she projected over the camera directly to me, the watcher. Loved watching her catch the frying pan as it almost went off the counter; loved her looking for the cover of the casserole. It was fascinating to watch her hand motions, which were so firm and sure with the food.[1]

The pilot episodes were a hit, and taping for the full 26-episode series began in January 1963. The first episode, broadcast on Monday, February 11, at 8:00 P.M., featured one of her classic dishes, *boeuf bourguignon*. It was an inspired selection. By choosing this dish, which is really just a French beef stew, Child was demonstrating that French cooking wasn't as "foreign" as it might sound, and not nearly as intimidating. And, perhaps most importantly for Child, the viewer could take the techniques learned from this episode and use them with a wide range of other dishes as well.

## MAKING A STEW, PUTTING ON A SHOW

Putting together a cooking show is much more difficult than it looks. Child worked and reworked the script, cooked and recooked the stew, figuring out the timing for each step of the recipe and learning how to work her way through the television kitchen. Due to budget constraints, the show would have be filmed straight through in one take—any errors, misspoken words, spilled dishes, or dropped food would have to be handled by Child as they happened. There would be no going back, no editing, and no retakes.

## IN HER OWN WORDS

Julia Child on the value of simplicity in cooking:

> You don't have to cook fancy or complicated masterpieces—just good food from fresh ingredients.*

---

* "Quote by Julia Child," GoodReads, http://www.goodreads. com/quotes/show/118657.

Within weeks of the premiere of *The French Chef*, audiences had become enamored with Julia Child. It was not just the recipes that were providing the attraction, however. The viewers appreciated Child for her personality, her joy for cooking, and her confidence.

Viewers sat entranced as black-and-white televisions across New England (this was before the wide use of color television) showed a close-up of a large covered casserole dish while the one-of-a-kind breathy voice of Julia Child proudly exclaimed, "Boeuf bourguignon! French beef stew in red wine!" Then, as a hand lifted the lid off the casserole, "We're going to serve it with braised onions, mushrooms, and wine-dark sauce. A perfectly delicious dish!"[2] Then finally, the camera followed a spoon coming from the casserole to the mouth of a woman, who tasted the finished dish.

After a serene smile of pleasure, she replaced the cover on the casserole, put it in the oven, and, much to the surprise of audiences watching, plopped a platter of raw meat on the counter. After looking into the wrong camera, she turned and looked into the right camera and briefly closed her eyes before proudly proclaiming, "Hello, I'm Julia Child."[3]

What followed was unlike anything ever shown on television before. Nervous when the show began taping, Child relaxed (as she always did) when she turned to the raw ingredients in hand and started to cook. After carefully showing the viewer at home the different cuts of beef that could be used in the dish (while demonstrating on her own body exactly where the cut came off the cow), she cut the meat into chunks, speaking directly to the television audience about the amount needed per person, all the while "handling the meat as affectionately as if she were powdering a baby."[4]

Then came one of the most crucial steps in preparing the stew—the browning of the beef. It was this lesson that demonstrated once and for all that television could be an ideal tool for teaching cooking to millions. It may seem that browning a piece of meat in a pan with hot fat is a simple

## DID YOU KNOW?

When Julia Child filmed the first episodes of *The French Chef*, she was only paid $50 per episode, plus a budget for ingredients. At that time, even members of her crew had never seen, much less tasted, ingredients such as leeks, artichokes, and even asparagus.

and basic procedure. But, as in anything else, there are more ways to do it wrong than to do it right—and only by doing it right could the dish be at its best.

Carefully and systematically, Child explained to the audience at home the things that could go wrong and how to avoid them, browning the meat properly while a mirror

## THE ANTI-JULIAS

On *The French Chef*, and in all of her subsequent television cooking shows, Julia Child preached the value of taking time to cook good food and using the best ingredients possible, saying that "convenience" could be a trap that emphasizes speed over quality. The pendulum, though, appears to have shifted, and many of today's most popular television chefs seem intent on preaching the gospel of fast and convenient, often at the expense of quality. In many ways, they seem to be a throwback to the kind of cooking and ideas about food that Child fought so hard against.

Take, for example, Rachael Ray and her show, *30-Minute Meals*. Many of her recipes are, legitimately, foods that can be made in 30 minutes: burgers and sandwiches, pastas, quick sautés of chicken, and the like. Other dishes, though, are 30-minute versions of dishes like boeuf bourguignon, which were never meant to be made in 30 minutes.

In Child's recipe, for example, after 30 to 45 minutes of prep time, the dish is slowly braised in the oven for 2.5 to 3 hours, time enough to bring out the best in all the ingredients and to allow the flavors to meld together into one harmonious whole. In Ray's version, in just 25 minutes from start to finish, the dish is on the table.

over the pan showed exactly what she was doing. As Laura Shapiro points out, "To a novice cook, or an experienced cook with bad habits, this lesson would have been life changing."[5]

After demonstrating how to deglaze the pan by pouring in red wine, allowing it to bubble up, and scraping the

Is Ray's version good? It's tasty, no doubt. Is it convenient for someone who has to get dinner on the table in a hurry? Without a doubt. Can it compare to the traditional recipe, with the rich depth of flavor that only careful preparation and slow cooking can provide? Doubtful.

The question, then, for the aspiring chef is this: Does the amount of time gained by cooking a 30-minute meal make up for the amount of flavor lost?

Then there's Sandra Lee of *Semi-Homemade Cooking with Sandra Lee* fame, whose philosophy is that by using 70 percent premade store-bought ingredients with 30 percent fresh, the viewer can create food that looks and tastes as though it was made from scratch. Take, for example, her recipe for Salisbury steak with mushroom gravy, which calls for, among other things ground beef, canned cream of mushroom soup, frozen chopped onions, and one packet of brown gravy mix.

One can only imagine what Child's reaction would be to a television show that did not try to inspire the viewer to work *harder* in the kitchen, to learn the skills necessary to become a good cook, but instead actually encouraged them to buy frozen prechopped onions rather than take the extra minute to peel and chop a fresh onion.

Julia Child chops squash while Paul photographs her for a cookbook. Paul and Julia Child were quite a team in putting together *The French Chef*, as he timed her during rehearsals and created diagrams to show the location of all the items needed for a particular episode. Each half-hour show required about 19 hours of work ahead of time.

bottom of the pan to release all the tasty brown bits known as "the fond" into the wine, she poured it over the meat in a casserole dish, making sure to note that the cook should add "just enough liquid so that the meat is barely covered. It's called *a fleur* in France. When the meat looks like little flowers."[6] She placed the dish in the oven to cook slowly, removing the casserole shown at the beginning of the program to again let the audience see what the completed dish should look like.

After recapping what the show had covered, and reminding viewers that the same techniques they had just learned could be used successfully with lamb, veal, or chicken, she signed off, after a bit of stumbling, with the words that would become her signature line: *Bon appétit*! (Meaning? "Enjoy your meal!")

The reaction was instantaneous and overwhelming—audiences throughout the area fell in love with Julia Child. Within two weeks, nearly 600 letters had arrived at the station, some asking for recipes, others simply offering their thanks for the cooking lesson. Child was pleased with the response, writing to William Koshland at Knopf that "I think we are luckily in at just the right time, as there have been no cooking shows for years, and people are evidently ripe for them."[7]

There was some truth to that—there had been an audience waiting and eager to learn how to prepare food that did not come from a box. But there was more to it as well. What people were responding to along with her cooking lessons was Child herself. Her personality, her joy in cooking, her confidence and happiness at being able to share what she had learned about cooking shone through the television, and viewers could not help falling in love with her and feeling that they knew her as a person, as the following excerpts from fan letters make clear:

We love her naturalness & lack of that T.V. manner, her quick but unhurried action, her own appreciation of what she is producing.

I love it where you say, "Oh, I forgot to tell you thus and so" (so *human* and *consoling* to amateur cooks.)

We love you, Julia!

Bernard Berenson wrote that there are two kinds of people, life-diminishing people and life-enhancing people. Certainly you must be the most life-enhancing person in America![8]

## PUTTING ON A SHOW IS HARD WORK

It may be difficult to believe, but Child often said that 19 hours of work went into each half-hour show. Every recipe had to be broken down into segments. Then, each step was rehearsed in her kitchen, while her husband, Paul, timed her on a stopwatch.

Each step had to be perfectly timed. For her show on making French onion soup, for example: How long did it take to chop a sample portion of onions while at the same time explaining to the viewer how to hold the knife? How long to melt the butter in the oil and start the onions browning? Each step had to be painstakingly worked out, not only the physical aspect but also what Child would say while demonstrating a particular technique or skill.

There was a script for each show, written up to display the time sequences, food, equipment needed, the procedures to be demonstrated, and what Child would say at each step. Each item that was going to be shown or even mentioned on air (the temperature of the oven, the number of pots of boiling water, samples of vegetables shown in their peeled and unpeeled states, the jars of spices, even equipment such as spatulas) had to be listed on the chart in the order that they would be discussed and used.

Dishes had to be precooked and ready to be shown on-air, everything from the completed dish to the ingredients shown in progressive stages of readiness. Paul Child, happily retired from the Foreign Service but now working full time alongside his wife, assisted in every way he could, including creating diagrams for each program that depicted the TV kitchen from Julia's perspective as she looked at the camera, showing precisely where every utensil, every ingredient, everything she would be using would be found when taping began.

On rehearsal days, the couple would get up at 6:00 A.M. to load the station wagon with all the precooked and partially cooked food, the equipment needed for that day's episode, the charts, and on special occasions, diagrams such as the one that Paul had worked on until two in the morning of a beef carcass, carefully illustrating the bone structure and all the classic cuts of beef.

Rehearsals would last all day and often into the night, as Child and the show's producer, Ruth Lockwood, blocked out the timing, camera movements, and all the other details that went into a show. As the two women worked, it fell to Paul Child to wash the continuous flow of dishes coming from the set. After everything was finalized, the Childs would repack the car, drive home, and unpack the car, after which Julia would make dinner and relax with a shot of bourbon, followed by bed.

On the days the show was taped, the procedure was repeated, with the addition of crew members busy setting up cameras, lights, and equipment around the kitchen set. Two shows were taped in succession. After the first, the crew would sit down to eat the food that Julia had prepared, while Paul did the dishes. Then another setup with different food and equipment, another 28-minute taping, followed by another trip home, bourbon, dinner, and bed.

Shooting four episodes a week made for an exhausting schedule. The show was so stressful to produce, with so much crammed into each segment, that the members of the production team often claimed that they aged 10 years with each show. With each episode, Child got better, growing more comfortable in front of the camera, knowing to wipe the sweat off her face while the camera was showing a close-up of the sauté pan, for example, and learning not to rush

By 1965, all 90 public-television stations across the country were carrying *The French Chef*, and Julia Child was a star. That year, she appeared in a TV special with White House chef Henry Haller, preparing a meal for President Lyndon B. Johnson.

from one part of the set to another. Within six months, Paul Child was proud to write in a letter to his brother that his wife was getting quite good at what she was doing.

And even more importantly, audiences loved what she was doing. Letters continued to flood into the station, praising the show and her. The *Boston Globe* ran an editorial calling the show "the talk of New England"[9] and hired her as a regular food columnist.

The show's impact, though, went way beyond that. When Child prepared a recipe in a certain kind of stoneware dish, for example, or used a certain kind of ring mold, kitchenware stores would not be able to keep those items in stock. And with the program's unprecedented popularity throughout New England, other public-television stations, including those in New York, San Francisco, Sacramento, Pittsburgh, and Washington, D.C., began to broadcast the show.

Wherever the show was broadcast, it received the same acclaim, the same flood of letters, the same demand for kitchenware, the same demand that grocery stores begin to carry items like fresh herbs, mushrooms, and other ingredients that were rarely found in stores in the 1960s.

Articles about Julia Child and *The French Chef* began to run in magazines nationwide, including *Time*, *Newsweek*, *TV Guide*, and the *Saturday Evening Post*. By January 1965, each of the 90 public-television stations across the country were showing *The French Chef*, and the show's home station, WGBH, even discovered it could make money by selling tickets to the show's tapings. Without a doubt, Child had become a star.

## WHAT MADE HER A STAR?

She was a star, and remained one for the next 40 years. Television audiences and readers alike responded to her skill as a teacher, her obvious passion for food, and her ability to give her audience the confidence that they, too, could learn to prepare good food.

Viewers were also responding to Julia Child herself. They loved it when she lifted a heavy cleaver high overhead and brought it down with a "whack" on a piece of meat. They loved it when, while preparing the fish stew known as bouillabaisse, she placed a gigantic fish head on the counter and kept it there for the entire show, occasionally lifting it up to hold it, showing the audience her love for the ingredients she was using.

They loved it that she obviously loved her own food. They loved it that, just like them, she tasted as she cooked. On one occasion, after demonstrating the art of folding beaten egg whites into the chocolate batter to help lighten it for a *reine de Saba* cake (a chocolate and almond cake, named after the Queen of Sheba, which Child described in *Mastering the Art of French Cooking* as "this extremely good chocolate cake"[10]), she paused with spatula in hand. Child then said, in that distinctive voice of hers, while looking directly into the camera, "We have this little bit on the edge of the spatula which is for the cook. That's part of the recipe."[11] How could anyone watching not fall in love with her?

It was, though, a love blended with respect. Audiences respected the fact that Child never "dumbed down" her recipes and never spoke down to her audience. While she made it clear that cooking was not necessarily easy, she also stressed that anyone could learn to cook who really wanted to and was willing to take the time.

Take the show demonstrating how to prepare the *reine de Saba* cake. By watching Child, viewers were taken carefully through each step of the recipe and were able to see how the texture of the batter changed with the addition of each ingredient. They were able to learn that, while melting chocolate over a pan of hot water might be tricky, it can be done with care and patience.

She showed people that cooking was both an art and a skill, and that it required, as she had learned from Chef Bugnard, the use of all of one's senses. There was no more accurate tool in the kitchen, she felt, than a cook who knew what to watch for, who knew what something was supposed to smell like, who knew what something was supposed to *taste* like.

Using a measuring spoon to measure spices accurately was important, but so too was knowing what a teaspoon of salt felt like in one's hand. Using a thermometer to check the temperature of a sugar syrup for making candied orange peel was important. But just as important, Child felt, was learning what the syrup should *sound* like and look like as it cooked. She told viewers that they could use a thermometer, "but I think it's a good thing to see and feel how it is."[12]

By showing people that cooking and eating well was not only possible but was also an essential part to living a good life, by teaching people the joy of cooking and then *showing* them that joy just by being herself, Julia Child had become a best-selling author and a television star by 1965 and had created a life and career for herself that would have been unimaginable just 10 years earlier. Few people, though, are able to stay at the top for long. Careers come and go, and today's star can easily become tomorrow's forgotten personality. Could the same thing happen to Julia Child?

# Icon and
# Legend

In 1965, Julia Child, 53 years old, was at the top of her profession. The career-defining, life-defining one-two punch of *Mastering the Art of French Cooking* and *The French Chef* had put her on top of America's culinary landscape. Her influence, her campaign to get Americans to appreciate food and cook seriously and from their heart was being felt in kitchens throughout the country. And, America had fallen in love with Child herself. How long could all of this last?

The answer is that it lasted until the day she died. For the next 40 years, Julia Child remained the ultimate television chef, appearing in one series after another: *Julia Child & Company, Julia Child & More Company, Dinner at Julia's, Cooking with Master Chefs: Hosted by Julia Child, In Julia's*

*Kitchen with Master Chefs, Baking with Julia*, and finally, *Julia & Jacques Cooking at Home*.

As many have pointed out, America, through Child's series and other television appearances, had the opportunity to watch her evolve as a chef and to grow old before its eyes. America watched Child go from an energetic woman in the prime of her life, whose larger-than-life physical presence seemed to fill the screen, to an elderly woman, smaller and slightly hunched over, who continued to charm and educate her audience while sitting back and letting her guest chefs do most of the cooking.

Her age simply did not seem to matter. In America's eyes, she would always be the cleaver-wielding, physically imposing, impossibly cheerful chef whose image had been established in the 1960s and 1970s. As Laura Shapiro put it, "This was the Julia who won a permanent place in the nation's memory bank."[1]

It was also that Julia Child who remained, throughout her career, a strict protector of her public image. It was her husband, Paul, who did all the photography for her shows and whose goal it was that the photographs that appeared of her in the press were ones that he had taken. Who else, he thought, would take the care to make sure that his wife, who was not necessarily the most photogenic person in the world, would always look her best? The public was also not privy to the information that she often went on diets to control her weight, that she wore a wig, and that, in 1971, she had a complete face-lift.

But there was more that went into controlling and protecting her image. Unlike many of today's television chefs, Child made it a rule *never* to endorse a product or promote a restaurant. "I just don't want to be in any way associated with commercialism (except for selling the book in a dignified way), and don't want to get into the realm of being a piece of property trotting about hither and yon," she said. "The line is sometimes difficult to see, but I know where I mean it to be."[2]

Despite the attempt to control the way she presented herself in public, life, or life in front of the camera, got in the way. By the mid-1960s, Child felt completely comfortable in front of the camera, so comfortable in fact that she acted there as she did in her own kitchen. And so, with the cameras rolling, she treated mistakes, goofs, and errant equipment with an ease that, despite not always presenting her in the best light possible, always charmed her viewers.

In fact, many people's strongest memories of Child are of her more than occasional, and all too human, fumbles in the kitchen. There was the time that she was attempting to unmold a *tarte tatin*—an apple tart that is baked with the fruit on the bottom in a caramel with the crust on top. When the tarte is done baking, it is flipped over so that a crispy, flaky crust is now on the bottom and the apples are in a brown, buttery, sweet sauce on top.

When Child tried to unmold her tarte tatin on camera, the whole thing collapsed, leaving her with messy piles of fruit and crust—just as it might happen in anyone's kitchen. Instead of making excuses, though, or panicking, she simply said, "That was a little loose. But I'll just have to show you that it's not going to make too much of a difference, because it's all going to fix up."[3]

Child did some quick repair work and then carried the unfortunate tart into the dining room set along with another tart, premade and perfect. "Now everybody can get one of each tart," she said, adding, "I think that actually makes a more interesting dessert."[4] Obviously, Child's early dictum to "never apologize" for your mistakes still held true.

The most famous of her on-air mistakes has since crossed over from fact into legend. Viewers claim to remember that it happened with a chicken, with several chickens, even with a 25-pound (11-kilogram) turkey. None of the above is true, but what actually happened is just as funny, just as memorable, and just as revealing of what Julia Child was all about.

## "YOU'RE ALONE IN THE KITCHEN— WHO IS GOING TO SEE?"

It occurred during the taping of a show all about potatoes. On the stove in a skillet was a large mashed potato cake, nearly brown on the bottom, waiting to be flipped. Time was running short, and even though Child was not certain that the cake was ready to be flipped, she decided to be brave and go ahead. Addressing the camera, she said, "When you flip anything you just have to have the courage of your convictions, particularly if it's sort of a loose mass, like this."[5] Then she gave the pan a sharp jerk.

As she obviously anticipated, the cake was not quite ready for its close-up. It fell apart in mid-air, half of it landing back in the pan, the other half falling in pieces all around the stove. "Well," she calmly noted, "that didn't go very well. You see, when I flipped it, I didn't have the courage to do it the way I should have."[6] Moving ahead smoothly she scooped up as much of the potato as she could and put it back together in the pan. "You're alone in the kitchen—who is going to see? But the only way you learn how to flip things is just to flip them."[7]

Viewers, naturally, laughed when they witnessed Child's potato cake disaster. In fact, critics remarked that she was often funnier than any professional comedienne. Paul Child even complained in a letter to his brother that "practically every article on Julie so far has concentrated on the clown instead of the woman, the cook, the expert or the revolutionary."[8]

Indeed, the image of Julia Child as a kitchen clown was only solidified when, on the television comedy show

On *Saturday Night Live*, Dan Aykroyd appeared in a skit as Julia Child, who bleeds profusely after cutting herself while preparing a chicken. Child, who had a good sense of humor about herself, loved the sketch and occasionally acted it out, too.

*Saturday Night Live*, Dan Aykroyd portrayed Child in a skit cutting up a chicken, then cutting herself and slowly bleeding to death, all the while urging viewers to "Save the liver!" The real Julia Child loved the sketch and kept a videotape of it to show friends who might never have seen it. On special occasions, she would even reenact the skit herself—playing Dan Aykroyd playing her, staggering around her office, and ending the skit "by sprawling herself across her desk and exclaiming, 'And then I died!' "[9]

Child was able to take the jokes about herself and laugh harder than anyone else. She knew that humor and entertainment could be used to make French cooking less intimidating for the home cook. But at the same time, for her, cooking was always a serious matter.

She often told viewers, "Cooking is one failure after another, and that's how you finally learn."[10] That was exactly how she had learned: Years of failure, followed by the right teacher, constant practice, and then success. That was what she hoped to teach Americans. So what if your omelet does not turn out perfect the first time? Get ahold of yourself, reread the recipe, figure out what went wrong, and try again. You will learn. Her line, "You're alone in the kitchen—who is going to see?," was more than just a line. It was her way of encouraging people to be brave in the kitchen, to be unafraid of making mistakes. She made them, and she was Julia Child. If they happened to her, they could happen to anyone.

## A GOOD LIFE

Her life had been everything she could ever have wanted. She was doing something she loved. She had achieved financial freedom. And, she was married to a man she truly loved. The two were a perfect partnership, not only as a married couple, but as business partners as well. When Child said that they did everything together, she meant it. And interestingly, as time went on, their roles slowly reversed.

For the first 15 years of their marriage, she had been Mrs. Paul Child, happily helping her husband with his career. Now, the tables were reversed, and, in some ways, he became Mr. Julia Child, known because of his famous wife, his life happily devoted to helping his wife with her career.

Paul Child was with her through every aspect of her career—attending business meetings and making his voice heard on everything, reworking recipes, moving equipment, taking photographs, helping her answer letters from fans, writing the dedications to her books, accompanying her on her publicity tours, lending her his expertise on wines.

They remained truly and deeply in love. The Childs were known for the Valentine's Day cards they sent out every year instead of Christmas cards (one of which famously included a photograph of Paul and Julia in a bubble bath). They made a point of snuggling together in bed every morning for a half hour after the alarm went off, and in the evening, while Julia was making dinner, Paul would read to her from *The New Yorker* magazine. "We are never not together," Paul often exclaimed happily.[11]

Paul and Julia Child had achieved what she called "that lovely intertwining of life, mind, and soul that a good marriage is."[12] Using the earnings from *Mastering the Art of French Cooking*, they were able to build a home in France, on property owned by Simca Beck right next to Beck's country home. La Pitchoune, as it was called, became their favorite retreat, a place where they could go to unwind from career pressures, relax in the country, enjoy the company of Beck, and enjoy, as only they could, life in France.

But while Julia still loved France and French cooking (in a 1966 interview with *Time* magazine, she said, "I will never do anything but French cooking. It is much the most interesting and the most challenging and the best

"We are never not together," Paul Child once said about him and Julia Child. Their love endured throughout their marriage, and they were known for sending out cards for Valentine's Day rather than Christmas.

eating"[13]), as time went on, her cooking changed as well. Other influences began to be seen. On one episode of *The French Chef*, she prepared a dish of spaghetti tossed with chopped walnuts, olives, pimento, and basil, naming the dish "spaghetti Marco Polo" and urging her viewers to eat it with chopsticks.

The book that many consider her magnum opus, *The Way to Cook*, published in 1989, included in-depth, detailed recipes for such non-French dishes as hamburgers, New England clam chowder, and Boston baked beans. It even included suggestions for low-calorie cooking, an idea that was ignored in *Mastering the Art of French Cooking*. While Child loved traditional French cooking, she was not limited to it and was willing to incorporate new ideas and trends into her cooking.

Then again, for Child, French cooking did not necessarily mean French recipes. To her, French cooking meant thinking about food in the way that the French did: "Taking ordinary everyday ingredients, and with a little bit of love and imagination, turning them into something appealing."[14] Indeed, with the end of her first television series, *The French Chef*, in 1973, the word "French" was no longer used in the titles of her books or her television shows.

In many ways, she had come full circle. Growing up eating "everyday" American food, she had escaped to France, where she learned to cook in the French way. She had learned and never stopped believing that the only culinary technique that mattered *was* French. Why? Because, as she often explained, "French cuisine was the only one that had precise terminology and definite rules, an actual body of knowledge to be taught. Once you learned the rules, you could apply them to any other cuisine in the world."[15]

She was confident enough in her abilities to be able to apply the techniques she had learned to the cuisine she had grown up eating, elevating it from something you had to eat to something you wanted to eat. *The Way to Cook*, for example, devotes five pages to making the perfect burger. This was what she wanted to teach the world: With good ingredients and proper technique, anything, even the simplest hamburger, can be made exquisite.

## LATER YEARS

The last years of Julia Child's life were a blend of career triumph and personal sorrow and loss. In her career as America's favorite television chef, she moved easily from success to success, slowly becoming seen less as a "real person" than as a legend and an icon. Unfortunately, in terms of personal life, she was still a real person, one who was forced to spend her final years without the company of her beloved husband, Paul.

His health, following heart surgery and a series of strokes, began a slow and inevitable decline. Julia adjusted as best she could, traveling less, hiring more staff to take up the work he was no longer able to do, giving up their beloved home in France, and splitting their time between their longtime home in Cambridge and a winter home in Santa Barbara, California. Finally, though, even Child's devotion to her husband wasn't enough.

Paul Child was placed in a nursing home in 1989 so he could get the full-time care he needed. He died there five years later, at age 92. Julia Child, for the first time in 48 years, was on her own.

There was, of course, her work, always her work. But she too was getting older and wasn't always in the best of health, so her last television series were filmed in the kitchen of her home in Cambridge. And instead of doing the cooking herself, she mostly watched as other guest chefs cooked, leaving Child to explain as only she could what they were doing and why they were doing it.

When she turned 80 in 1992, a full year of celebrations were held throughout the culinary world. More than 300 parties were thrown around the country, and Child, despite her age and health, attended nearly all of them. WGBH, the Boston public-television station that launched her career, threw a party in Boston, complete with stars from the worlds of food and the arts, along with the famous Boston Pops Orchestra performing a piece written especially for the occasion, "Fanfare with Pots and Pans," played, naturally enough, with pots, pans, whisks, and wooden spoons.

Fourteen of the nation's best chefs prepared a special tribute dinner at the Rainbow Room in New York City. At the Ritz-Carlton in Marina del Rey, California, nine French chefs were flown in to prepare a multi-course banquet for Child along with 60 top American chefs. Smaller private parties were held at restaurants and homes across the United States, all prepared by chefs, some professional, some not, whose cooking and life Child had influenced. It is difficult, indeed, to imagine a more fitting gift for her on her birthday than to *cook* for her, to repay, in some small way, all that cooking, all the fine food, she had given them.

## JULIE & JULIA

It all began in 2002 when Julie Powell, a young woman living in New York City and trapped in a job she did not enjoy, tried to find a way to enliven her life. What she decided to do was methodically work her way through Julia Child's classic cookbook, *Mastering the Art of French Cooking*, preparing every recipe in it over the course of a year. To document her progress, she started a blog, "The Julie/Julia Project," on the Web site Salon.com.

The blog took off, and a growing audience of readers began to follow Powell's progress, her triumphs, and her mistakes. Publishers took notice, and in 2005 Little, Brown and Company published the results of her experiment as the book *Julie & Julia: 365 Days, 524 Recipes, 1 Tiny Apartment Kitchen*. (The paperback edition was retitled *Julie and Julia: My Year of Cooking Dangerously*.)

With the book a success, it was no surprise that Hollywood purchased the film rights to the project. Written and directed by Nora Ephron, the resulting film combines two stories: the story of Julie Powell as told in her book and that of Julia Child as she recounted in her own autobiography, *My Life in France*. By alternating between the two stories—Child's life in France and her success in finding herself by learning to cook and struggling to write and publish *Mastering the Art of French Cooking*,

Tributes continued to come in, including the French Legion of Honor in 2000 and the U.S. Presidential Medal of Freedom in 2003. Child herself, though, was beginning to fade. In 2001, she moved into a retirement community in Santa Barbara, donating her home and office in Cambridge to Smith College and donating her now-famous kitchen,

and Powell's struggle to find herself as well, by working her way through that same cookbook—both stories were made richer and more meaningful.

The movie, which starred Meryl Streep as Julia Child, Amy Adams as Julie Powell, and Stanley Tucci as Paul Child, premiered on July 30, 2009, at New York City's Ziegfeld Theatre before opening throughout North America on August 7, 2009. The movie, titled *Julie & Julia*, received good notices, but reviewers fell over themselves praising Streep's performance as Child, noting that while she captured Child's physical mannerisms perfectly, she went way beyond that, capturing the very essence of Child herself.

*Julie & Julia* was a huge box-office success, but its impact went beyond that. One month after the movie's release, and almost 48 years after it was published, for the first time in its history, *Mastering the Art of French Cooking* hit the number-one position on the *New York Times* best-seller list. Once again, Julia Child (as played by Meryl Streep, with the assistance of Julie Powell, as played by Amy Adams) was encouraging Americans to stop by a bookstore on their way home from the theater, go home, and start cooking. Julia Child would, undoubtedly, have been very pleased.

In 1992, the year Julia Child turned 80, the culinary world held a year-long celebration, with more than 300 parties thrown in her honor. During one event, Child sang with chefs (*from left*) Roberto Donna, Jean-Louis Palladin, Bob Kinkead, Jim Sands, and Will Greenwood.

the set for three of her television series, to the Smithsonian's National Museum of American History.

## FOOD AND LEGACY

In her later years, Child was often asked what she would like for her last meal. The answer varied: On many occasions she said she would like to start with oysters, followed by a roast duck, a salad, one perfectly ripe pear, and just a bite of chocolate. On another occasion, when asked by restaurateur George Lang about her last meal, she gave a much more detailed response.

The most important aspect, she felt, was that the meal should be cooked at her own home, along with one or two friends whom she enjoyed cooking with. There should be no more than six people at the table. They would start with Cotuit oysters, along with very thinly sliced, buttered, homemade rye bread. Caviar and vodka would follow, then "some very fresh, fine, green California asparagus."[16] The main course would be one of her very favorite dishes, roast duck, served with a port wine sauce. There would be fresh green peas, and *pommes Anna*, a dish of thinly sliced layered potatoes, cooked in a large amount of butter so that the bottom of the dish is nicely crispy.

Naturally there would be a great wine, a simple salad of lettuce and endive with just lemon juice and French olive oil for the dressing, sprinkled with a few toasted walnuts. There would be cheese and great bread, charlotte malakoff (a particularly luscious almond cream) for dessert, along with grapes and pears, finally ending with chocolate truffles and coffee. "At least that meal would suit me now," she said, "and probably would then, at the very end, before we all slipped off the raft."[17]

## IN HER OWN WORDS

Julia Child on what was important in her life:

> I don't think about whether people will remember me or not. I've been an okay person. I've learned a lot. I've taught people a thing or two. That's what's important.*

---

* "Julia McWilliams Child, 1912–2004," http://www.qotd.org/search/search.html?aid=3986.

Life, though, does not always end as we would like. On August 10, 2004, having survived kidney failure, a stroke, and painful knee surgery, for the last time in her life, Child was pushed in a wheelchair into her kitchen and helped chop onions for a French onion soup her assistant Stephanie was preparing, using the recipe from her own *Mastering the Art of French Cooking*. It was the last meal she ever ate.

The next day, although her doctor had told her that she had developed an infection and needed to be hospitalized, Child decided to refuse treatment. Stephanie helped her get settled in her bed, and with her cat Minou lying on the covers next to her, she fell asleep and never woke up. She died two days later of kidney failure, just two days shy of her ninety-second birthday.

Although Julia Child did, in her own words, get off to a late start, once she did, she made the most of it. It can safely be said that, by the time she hit her 50s, she was a woman who had it all. She had a husband she adored and who adored her back. She had found her passion, a love for food and cooking, that brought her the deepest of satisfactions. To top it all off, she found a way to turn that passion into a career and, in the process, share that passion with the world. In turn, that passion changed the way Americans thought about food, about cooking, and how food and cooking, if one pays attention, can change one's life, just as it did hers.

As she said at the end of her autobiography, *My Life in France*:

> In Paris in the 1950s, I had the supreme good fortune to study with a remarkably able group of chefs. From them I learned why good French food is an art, and why it makes such sublime eating: nothing is too much trouble if it turns out the way it should. Good results require that one take *time*

and *care*. If one doesn't use the freshest ingredients or read the whole recipe before starting, and if one rushes through the cooking, the result will be an inferior taste and texture. . . . But a careful approach will result in a magnificent burst of flavor, a thoroughly satisfying meal, perhaps even a life-changing experience.[18]

For showing us how to cook well, to eat well, and to live well, we all owe Julia Child our thanks. And, as she would say, *bon appétit*!

# CHRONOLOGY

1912    Julia Child is born Julia Carolyn McWilliams on August 15 in Pasadena, California.

1934    Graduates from Smith College in Northampton, Massachusetts (her mother's alma mater), with a degree in history and no career plans.

1942    During World War II, Julia goes to work for the U.S. Information Center in Washington, D.C., before transferring to the Office of Strategic Services (OSS).

1944    Julia requests and receives a transfer overseas, ending up in Kandy, Ceylon, where her assignment is to set up and operate the Registry. While there, she meets Paul Child, 10 years her senior.

1945    Along with Paul Child, she is transferred to Kunming, China. When the war ends, Julia returns to Pasadena, and Paul to Washington, D.C.

1946    After months of correspondence and a cross-country road trip, Julia McWilliams and Paul Child marry on September 1. They set up house in Washington, D.C.

1948    Paul Child is sent to France as part of the U.S. Information Service. Driving from Le Havre to Paris, the couple stops for lunch at Restaurant Le Couronne, where Julia has the meal that inspires her love of food and cooking.

1949    She attends Le Cordon Bleu.

1952    Along with Simone Beck and Louisette Bertholle, she starts a cooking school in Paris that they call L'Ecole des Trois Gourmandes.

1952    Beck and Bertholle ask for help in translating into English a French cookbook they had been working on for several years. After looking over the manuscript, Child agrees to take on the project as a coauthor, if Beck and Bertholle agree to a complete rewrite. They do.

1952–1960    The cookbook, designed to be the most complete cookbook of French cooking and technique available, is worked and reworked. The book goes through two publishers before it is accepted for publication by Alfred A. Knopf in May 1960.

1961    *Mastering the Art of French Cooking* is published and receives rave reviews.

1963    *The French Chef* premieres in February on WGBH, Boston's public-television station. Within two years, the show is being broadcast nationwide.

1964    Julia Child receives the prestigious George Foster Peabody Award for *The French Chef*.

1968    *The French Chef Cookbook* is published.

1970    *Mastering the Art of French Cooking, Volume Two*, is published.

| | |
|---|---|
| 1975 | *From Julia Child's Kitchen* is published. |
| 1978–1979 | The television series *Julia Child & Company* runs, and a companion cookbook of the same name is published. |
| 1980–1982 | The television series *Julia Child & More Company* airs, and a companion cookbook of the same name is published. |
| 1981 | Julia Child, along with Robert Mondavi and Richard Graff, cofounds the "American Institute of Wine and Food." |
| 1983–1985 | The television series *Dinner at Julia's* runs. |
| 1986 | Child cofounds the James Beard Foundation. |
| 1989 | *The Way to Cook* is published. |
| 1993–1994 | The television series *Cooking with Master Chefs: Hosted by Julia Child* airs, and a companion cookbook of the same name is published. |
| 1994 | Paul Child dies. |
| 1994–1996 | The television series *In Julia's Kitchen with Master Chefs* runs, and a companion cookbook is published. |
| 1996–1998 | The television series *Baking with Julia* is shown, and a companion cookbook of the same name is published. |
| 1999–2000 | The television series *Julie and Jacques Cooking at Home* airs, and a companion cookbook of the same name is published. |
| 2000 | *Julia's Kitchen Wisdom* is published. France awards Julia Child with the Chevalier of |

the Légion d'Honneur—the Legion of Honor.

2001    Child moves from Cambridge, Massachusetts, to Santa Barbara, California; she donates her kitchen to the Smithsonian.

2003    She is awarded the U.S. Presidential Medal of Freedom.

2004    Julia Child dies in her sleep on Friday, August 13, just two days before her ninety-second birthday, of kidney failure.

# NOTES

## CHAPTER 1

1. Julia Child with Alex Prud'homme, *My Life in France*. New York: Anchor Books, 2007, p. 261.
2. Ibid.
3. Laura Shapiro, *Julia Child: A Life*. New York: Penguin Books, 2007, p. 100.
4. Ibid., p. xiv.
5. Child, *My Life in France*, p. 3.

## CHAPTER 2

1. Noël Riley Fitch, *Appetite for Life: The Biography of Julia Child*. New York: Anchor Books, 1999, p. 13.
2. Child, *My Life in France*, p. 83.
3. Fitch, *Appetite for Life*, p. 14.
4. Shapiro, *Julia Child*, p. 1.
5. Fitch, *Appetite for Life*, p. 23.
6. Ibid., p. 17.
7. Ibid., p. 24.
8. Ibid., p. 31.
9. Ibid., p. 33.
10. Ibid., pp. 43–44.
11. Shapiro, *Julia Child*, p. 4.
12. Fitch, *Appetite for Life*, p. 59.
13. Ibid., p. 64.
14. Ibid., p. 65.
15. Ibid., p. 66.
16. Ibid., p. 68.
17. Shapiro, *Julia Child*, p. 5.
18. Fitch, *Appetite for Life*, pp. 72–73.
19. Shapiro, *Julia Child*, p. 6.
20. Fitch, *Appetite for Life*, p. 77.
21. Shapiro, *Julia Child*, p. 9.
22. Ibid., p. 8.

## CHAPTER 3

1. Shapiro, *Julia Child*, p. 9.
2. Ibid., p. 12.
3. Ibid.
4. Ibid., p. 14.
5. Fitch, *Appetite for Life*, pp. 95–96.
6. Shapiro, *Julia Child*, p. 17.
7. Fitch, *Appetite for Life*, p. 106.
8. Ibid., p. 115.
9. Ibid., p. 121.
10. Ibid., p. 124.
11. Ibid., p. 130.
12. Shapiro, *Julia Child*, p. 24.
13. Ibid., p. 26.
14. Fitch, *Appetite for Life*, p. 142.
15. Ibid., p. 143.
16. Ibid., p. 148.
17. Ibid., p. 150.

## CHAPTER 4

1. Julia Child, *From Julia Child's Kitchen*. New York: Alfred A. Knopf, 1975, p. 117.
2. Fitch, *Appetite for Life*, p. 156.
3. Shapiro, *Julia Child*, p. 29.
4. Ibid., p. 31.
5. Ibid.
6. Ibid., p. 32.
7. Child, *My Life in France*, p. 61.
8. Ibid., p. 62.
9. Shapiro, *Julia Child*, p. 33.
10. Ibid., pp. 33–34.
11. Ibid., p. 35.
12. Ibid., p. 37.
13. Child, *My Life in France*, p. 64.

14. Ibid.
15. Ibid., p. 65.
16. Ibid.
17. Ibid.
18. Ibid., p. 68.
19. Ibid.
20. Shapiro, *Julia Child*, p. 38.
21. Ibid.
22. Ibid., p. 40.
23. Ibid.
24. Ibid., p. 41.
25. Ibid.
26. Ibid., p. 43.
27. Ibid.
28. Ibid., p. 45.

## CHAPTER 5

1. Child, *My Life in France*, p. 146.
2. Ibid., p. 149.
3. Ibid.
4. Ibid., p. 150.
5. Ibid.
6. Shapiro, *Julia Child*, p. 55.
7. Ibid.
8. Child, *My Life in France*, p. 247.
9. Ibid., p. 225.
10. Shapiro, *Julia Child*, p. 81.
11. Ibid.
12. Ibid., p. 83.
13. Ibid., pp. 83–84.
14. Ibid., p. 85.
15. Child, *My Life in France*, p. 231.

## CHAPTER 6

1. Shapiro, *Julia Child*, p. 86.
2. Child, *My Life in France*, p. 238.
3. Ibid.
4. Ibid., p. 240.
5. Ibid., p. 245.
6. Ibid., p. 249.
7. Ibid., p. 253.
8. Shapiro, *Julia Child*, p. 94.
9. Ibid., p. 95.

## CHAPTER 7

1. Shapiro, *Julia Child*, p. 100.
2. Ibid., pp. 101–102.
3. Ibid., p. 102.
4. Ibid., pp. 102–103.
5. Ibid., p. 103.
6. Ibid.
7. Ibid., p. 104.
8. Ibid.
9. Ibid., p. 110.
10. Julia Child, Louisette Bertholle, and Simone Beck, *Mastering the Art of French Cooking*. New York: Alfred A. Knopf, 2009, p. 677.
11. Shapiro, *Julia Child*, p. 112.
12. Ibid., p. 113.

## CHAPTER 8

1. Shapiro, *Julia Child*, p. 111.
2. Ibid., p. 116.
3. Ibid., p. 118.
4. Ibid.

5. Ibid., pp. 118–119.
6. Ibid., p. 119.
7. Ibid.
8. Ibid., p. 120.
9. Nancy Verde Barr, *Backstage with Julia: My Years with Julia Child*, Hoboken, N.J.: Wiley & Sons, 2007, p. 80.
10. Shapiro, *Julia Child*, p. 121.
11. Ibid., p. 130.
12. Ibid., p. 133.
13. Ibid., p. 147.
14. Ibid., p. 148.
15. Ibid., p. 149.
16. Ibid., p. 175.
17. Ibid., p. 176.
18. Child, *My Life in France*, pp. 332–333.

# BIBLIOGRAPHY

Barr, Nancy Verde. *Backstage with Julia: My Years with Julia Child*. Hoboken, N.J.: Wiley & Sons, 2007.

Child, Julia. *From Julia Child's Kitchen*. New York: Alfred A. Knopf, 1975.

———. *The Way to Cook*. New York: Alfred A. Knopf, 2010.

Child, Julia, with Alex Prud'homme. *My Life in France*. New York: Anchor Books, 2007.

Child, Julia, Louisette Bertholle, and Simone Beck. *Mastering the Art of French Cooking*. New York: Alfred A. Knopf, 2009.

Fitch, Noël Riley. *Appetite for Life: The Biography of Julia Child*. New York: Anchor Books, 1999.

Fussell, Betty. *Masters of American Cookery: The American Food Revolution and the Chefs Who Shaped It*. New York: Times Books, 1983.

Saint-Ange, Madame E. *La Bonne Cuisine*. Berkeley, Calif.: Ten Speed Press, 2005.

Shapiro, Laura. *Julia Child: A Life*. New York: Penguin Books, 2007.

# FURTHER RESOURCES

## BOOKS

Brillat-Savarin, Jean Anthelme. *The Physiology of Taste: Or Meditations on a Transcendental Gastronomy*. New York: Everyman's Library, 2009.

Chamberlain, Samuel. *Clémentine in the Kitchen*. New York: Modern Library, 2001.

Child, Julia. *Julia's Kitchen Wisdom: Essential Techniques and Recipes from a Lifetime of Cooking*. New York: Alfred A. Knopf, 2009.

Fisher, M.F.K. *The Art of Eating*. Hoboken, N.J.: Wiley Publishing, 2004.

Kamp, David. *The United States of Arugula: The Sun-Dried, Cold-Pressed, Dark-Roasted, Extra Virgin Story of the American Food Revolution*. New York: Broadway Books, 2007.

Reardon, Joan. *M.F.K. Fisher, Julia Child, and Alice Waters: Celebrating the Pleasures of the Table*. New York: Harmony Books, 1994.

## WEB SITES

Julia Child's Kitchen at the Smithsonian
http://americanhistory.si.edu/juliachild

KQED: Julia Child
http://www.kqed.org/food/juliachild

PBS: Julia Child
http://www.pbs.org/juliachild

# PICTURE CREDITS

# INDEX

# ABOUT THE AUTHOR

DENNIS ABRAMS is the author of numerous books for Chelsea House, including biographies of Barbara Park, Xerxes, Rachael Ray, L. Frank Baum, Georgia O'Keeffe, Hillary Rodham Clinton, Eminem, and Nicolas Sarkozy. He attended Antioch College, where he majored in English and communications. He currently lives in Houston, Texas, with his partner of 21 years, three cats, and a dog named Junie B.